DIGITAL MARKETING IN AN AI WORLD

FREDERICK VALLAEYS

DIGITAL
MARKETING
IN AN
AI WORLD

FUTUREPROOFING YOUR PPC AGENCY

MODERN MARKETING MASTERS

DIGITAL MARKETING IN AN AI WORLD

Futureproofing Your PPC Agency

ISBN   978-1-5445-1337-9 *Paperback*

978-1-5445-1336-2 *Ebook*

CONTENTS

FOREWORD

Many industries go through a transition from manual labor to automation. The good news is that automation generally results in consistently better products, increased efficiency, and lower prices. The bad news is that it leads to layoffs, compressed margins, and product commoditization.

For search-engine marketers (SEM), advances in artificial intelligence (AI) and machine learning (ML) have led to a real possibility that the primary roles humans play today—ad creative, account structure, targeting, landing pages, bidding, keyword creation—will be automated over the next few years.

So, will human SEM experts be needed once these massive computers are crunching billions of datapoints to derive optimal SEM performance?

The answer is yes...and no. There's no question that automation will reduce the need for people in certain roles. Pay-per-click (PPC) agencies will be able to do the same amount of work with fewer people. But despite advances in our ability to create "smart" computers, we are still far away from computers that will completely displace humans.

First, we need humans to create and improve algorithms. Most ML is based on supervised learning, with people curating sample data sets. Moreover, computers make mistakes, so there will always be a need for humans to do quality assurance (QA) on results.

But humans will be needed for more than just routine error prevention. Humans can infer opportunity where a computer can't. For example, for a Super Bowl marketing campaign, we might consider that the Super Bowl is watched:

- by a lot of people
- at home
- with friends
- eating snacks
- the South Beach Diet is popular
- vegetables are low in carbs, and
- it's currently mushroom season

So, your agency should buy "mushroom" keywords!

The above example shows a highly complex process of deduction due to the variability of inputs leading to the conclusion. Think about it: in that paragraph, my mind processed information about technology, cultural habits, fads, nutrition, and vegetable seasonality. This sort of nonlinear thinking is difficult for computers to replicate.

Will computers continue to play a greater role in SEM? Absolutely! Will SEM experts be obsolete in the next five years? Not a chance.

My colleague and friend Fred Vallaeys's book will tell you much more about how and why. If you are a PPC professional or agency owner, read it!

DAVID RODNITZKY
CEO, 3Q DIGITAL

INTRODUCTION

Is the sky really falling? It sure seems to be. Announcements about AI's increasing importance in Google Ads have many PPC agencies and professionals confused, scared, and ducking for cover. After all, Google is by far the biggest player in pay-per-click (PPC) advertising. And yes: artificial intelligence, and specifically machine learning, are transforming the PPC landscape. But no: this does not mean that machines are ready to take over from us humans. In fact, the best results may happen when machines and humans work together.

There are many ways to futureproof your role as a PPC expert. However, the current changes do require you to reevaluate and refocus, and this book will tell you how.

When Google introduced AdWords in 2000, everything was done manually. Over time, Google layered more and more automation into the process. Working there from 2002 until 2012, first as a Product Specialist and then as the AdWords Evangelist—spreading the word about this new form of advertising—I saw all this happen from inside the company that invented online advertising as we know it today.

In 2016, Google CEO Sundar Pichai announced we would soon be living in an "AI-first world," and that Google was going to become an "AI-first company." Since then, machine intelligence has driven the changes that have produced a new generation of AdWords, which was rechristened Google Ads in July 2018. The push towards AI has many, perhaps most, PPC agencies and professionals wondering: what does this mean for me? Is the "AI-first" Google going to put me out of a job? Will the things I've been doing to make accounts successful, such as optimization and reporting, be handled by machines?

PPC angst is even stronger because so many digital marketers are fairly young, towards the beginning of their work lives. They may have thirty years of their careers left, and, in that case, what does the AI push mean for them? If you believe Google's official pronouncements, machines will be doing everything long before it's time to retire.

In this rapidly changing environment, the half-understood "artificial intelligence" jargon being thrown around only increases confusion. The media, seeing a trend, is now extensively covering this new, "disruptive" technology. Media dramatization of AI always seems to come down to the image of a beautiful humanoid robot—like Alicia Vikander in the movie *Ex Machina*—taking over from us poor humans.

However, the story of what's really happening is considerably less sexy—and less frightening. Machine learning is great at figuring out correlations within masses of data: indeed, it's a lot better at finding patterns in large data sets than we humans are. What this really means is we're seeing the increasing automation of the highly repetitive, boring, and tedious tasks of pulling data from reports and looking for signals within the noise. This is where machines, rather than people, excel.

Marketing, however, remains a fundamentally human field: communicating with other people, telling them what you can offer, and inspiring them to act. Intuition and creativity are at the foundation of much of our human intelligence. We've done pretty well as a species for quite a long time, and machines are not going to suddenly become better than humans at communication or creative intuition.

Yes, machine learning is having a considerable impact on PPC marketing. This has been true for some time and will be even more so in the future. At the moment, however, it appears that we're at an AI inflection point, which means it's more important than ever to separate fact from paranoid fiction and figure out what's really going on.

As one of Google's first 500 employees and its first AdWords Evangelist, I have great respect for the company and its products and services, some of which I helped create. However, I also feel they could do more to explain how humans and machines can successfully collaborate. Without guidance from the company most responsible for driving the AI revolution, they allow paranoia surrounding AI and PPC advertising to persist. Yes, CEO Sundar Pichai has said Google will be an "AI-first" company. What tends to happen in big companies is whatever the CEO says becomes gospel: this is what we're going to do!

This can reach the point of the absurd, as a *Wall Street Journal* article has described (https://www.wsj.com/articles/how-bosses-waste-their-employees-time-1534126140). At a breakfast meeting, a CEO commented that no blueberry muffins were available, although there were plenty of other things to eat, and he didn't particularly care for blueberry muffins. He was just making small talk about the food. Blueberry muffins began appearing at every breakfast meeting thereafter. It was several months before the CEO realized that a very casual remark on his part had been taken as a hard-and-fast requirement.

What's happening with Google Ads, now that the CEO has said they're an AI-first company? Two years ago, during Google's annual marketing event at which new products are launched, a product manager got up on stage and said: "In the past, you had to worry about which ads to write for which audiences. But now, our machine learning is smart enough that you can just submit fifty different ad variations, and the system will figure out which is the right one to show to each individual user."

The speaker's concrete example was a user looking for hotels. Google would already know if that particular user responds better to ads for inexpensive or for five-star hotels, or prefers results featuring a variety of different kinds of accommodations. The system then delivers the hotel ads the user will be most likely to click on. Since Google makes money from every click on an ad, there is a strong incentive to show the most clickable ads to every user every time a search happens. Hotels, of course, benefit too, because if the ads connect better with users, the rate of bookings per click—the conversion rate—is likely to be higher too.

In the last year, this process has intensified with the introduction of Google's new "smart" features: smart bidding, smart campaigns, smart shopping. "Smart" is basically just Google's new nomenclature for anything that's machine learning driven. Now, instead of being told that the machine will figure out which ads to show, as was the case two years ago, PPC professionals are being told: "Tell us how much money you're willing to spend, give us the site you want to drive the customer to, and let us handle everything else." The smart system will figure out how to get you the most conversions for your money.

The increase in how much Google is able to automate frightens many PPC professionals. In the past, it was the agency's job to figure out targeting, keywords, audiences, and the bidding process: how much the client should be willing to pay for each click. You would also have to determine negative keywords, bid adjustments, and much of what Google is now handling automatically in their "smart" campaigns. While these are important decisions, many are a function of math and statistics, which makes this element of PPC a prime point of automation. PPC pros, who are capable of much deeper thinking and strategy, should look in the mirror and ask what kind of PPC pro they really want to be.

From Google's perspective, this shift is quite real. There is an absolute move towards increased automation. But what this actually means is unrelated to the messages about AI the media tends to promote. When the media talks about artificial intelligence, it's generally not in the context of digital marketing. Instead, you'll probably hear stories about IBM's Watson doing a cancer diagnosis.

Will AI replace human doctors? (Hint: very unlikely.) Or, you hear about artificial intelligence getting really good at playing certain games, having mastered chess and, more recently, the still more complex game of Go. People envision a human sitting across the table from a machine that has all the human's capabilities and then some. This perception of AI is inconsistent with reality. People think that AI can—or will soon be able to—figure almost anything out much more easily and accurately than a human can. However, the reality today is AI can help humans get better insights more quickly, enabling smarter decisions.

As of early 2019, Google Ads "smart" machine learning solutions still tend to be very specific. They are point solutions, as is the case with AI in other industries and verticals. Smart bidding is all about bid optimization. Smart campaigns are about automatically figuring out ad targeting and how to allocate bids and budgets across different ad formats. Popular perception, bolstered by the media, seems to indicate that there is very little left for humans—you—to do. However, the company still offers several types of Google Ads campaigns in addition to "smart" ones. It's for the PPC professional to figure out if a smart campaign is really the way to go in a specific situation, and the answer is sometimes no. Well-managed but more manual campaign types, built on long-standing optimization principles, frequently still work more effectively.

If you decide to go the smart campaign route, it can seem there will be little hands-on management to be done after launch. Even with smart campaigns, though, you can almost always drive better results by setting up multiple campaigns with different goals and targets. Google itself acknowledges this in its documentation, which includes provisos such as: "you should have different target returns on ad spend for different campaigns, possibly based on promotions you may be running."

A hotel, for instance, may be running a reduced-rate special on what would otherwise be a slow weekend. While machine learning does what it does quite well, it may not realize you're running a special promotion for two days this coming weekend quickly enough. By the time the "smart" campaign figures it out, your sale is over. You've lost the opportunity for increased sales because the smart system didn't adjust your bids quickly enough. Human intervention was required.

The point is, even with "fully automated" solutions, there's still quite a bit of management involved. When PPC professionals add their own human experience, intelligence, and creativity to the "smart" system's recommendations, you get better results.

It's true Google is doing some amazing things using machine learning to make its PPC customers more successful. At the same time, people are worried about what Google might "really" be doing, and especially about where innovations in machine learning are leading. A PPC professional's first question is, "Am I going to lose my job?" An agency's question is, "Are we going to lose all our clients?" The answer is: "You'll have a job (and an agency) if you have the right skills." However, you need to learn what the right skills are—ones that machines can't replace—how to develop them, and how to position and market yourself and your agency. You'll also have a job, because machines plus humans can outperform machines acting alone. The machines can achieve average results without you in the mix, if that is what you aspire to. If you want stellar results, a strong process combining the best human with the best machine skills is required.

Most people come to the right conclusions if you give them the right information. One of Google's key tenets is transparency and information-sharing. The company's attitude is that trends don't need to be spelled out, they can be figured out. If you give intelligent people the same information, they'll generally come to similar conclusions.

Information-sharing is the reason I decided to write this book. PPC professionals need to find out what AI really is and how it really works. Once you begin to better understand the technology and its impact on PPC advertising, you'll be able to see your options far more clearly and can develop your own vision of how to benefit from, rather than be intimidated by, the technology. You'll realize how you can skill or re-skill yourself not only to survive but to thrive. The PPC professional who takes the proper action will still have a job.

Then how, as an agency owner, can you also make sure your clients will continue to use your company's services? You may be great at your job, but your clients are exposed to the same media you are, and many businesspeople are eager to try out whatever is "new and improved." A long-time client might come to you and say, "Well, I just read about Google smart campaigns in *Wired*. Why aren't we doing that? Why do I still pay a team of humans to do all these things, when artificial intelligence should be able to do it all a lot more cheaply?" How do you answer a question like that and make your value proposition clear? The truth is there are many ways to futureproof your agency, and futureproofing will be a main focus of the chapters that follow.

This book is in three parts. The first will help you better understand the specific roles artificial intelligence plays in PPC advertising, separating fact from fiction and what humans do best from what machines do best. The second part focuses on essential roles or personas—creative, client-facing, and technical—PPC professionals will continue to play, since AI can't. One of these roles will probably appeal to you more than the others, and that is where you will want to focus your energy. The third part deals with positioning and futureproofing your PPC agency in "an AI world." How do you frame or reframe your value proposition to clients eager to hop on the latest bandwagon, even if they have no idea where it's going?

The first part is background information about what PPC machine learning is. The second and third parts contain more actionable information about positioning or repositioning yourself or your agency in a machine learning world. Some of you may wish to go straight to part two or three, where the rubber meets the road. The part one background, however, will probably help you, the PPC professional, better understand the often-confusing trends dominating the industry today.

AdWords created the PPC industry. Rebranded as Google Ads, it is still by far the most powerful and influential force in the space. Because I was fortunate enough to be a key member of the AdWords team for many years, I'd like to start by giving you a front-row seat for a review of how machine learning was introduced and then became an evermore-integral part of PPC advertising. This will contextualize a concept—AI—that's often used vaguely and out of context. Learning more about the "AI-first"

PPC world, you'll be better able to position yourself to become one of its most productive citizens.

DIGITAL MARKETING TECHNOLOGY: SEPARATING FACT FROM FICTION

AI AND DIGITAL MARKETING: BACKGROUND

PPC professionals are confused about how AI is going to affect their business and their livelihoods. Is the end near at hand?

In my early days at Google AdWords, we were concerned our customers referred to our Quality Score (QS) system—an estimate of the relevance of their keywords, ads, and landing pages—as a black box. Our customers felt this way because they didn't know what they needed to do to achieve a high-quality score, and this lack of transparency was frustrating them.

People are afraid of what they don't understand, and fear makes them angry. So, over time, we made the QS as transparent as you can make a machine learning system. We made sure customers were better informed about how the system rated their choice of keywords, as well as the relevance of their ads and landing pages. When they understood it better, they made better optimizations, making advertisers, users, and Google all happier. More transparency led to a better alignment of incentives and better results for all.

QS was yesterday's black box; today's black box is AI or machine learning. People don't understand what machine learning is or what its impact on PPC advertising is going to be. What's required, again, is greater transparency. We PPC professionals need to get on the same page with a shared understanding of the current state of AI technology and arrive at some rational assumptions about where we are headed. Only by being better informed can PPC professionals independently formulate and come to an understanding of how AI matters to their businesses. Although the learning process is somewhat technical, it's still important.

FROM BELGIUM TO GOOGLE ADWORDS

First, let me tell you a bit about my background. How did I become a Google AdWords Evangelist?

I'm from Belgium and moved to California when I was

fifteen because my father had a job with Tandem Computers in Cupertino. I was very excited to be moving to Silicon Valley. I was completely into computers and knew that I was going to be living at ground zero of where the technologies that were changing the world were being invented.

I finished high school there and got into Stanford, which sealed the deal. I wanted to stay in Silicon Valley and didn't seriously consider any other schools. I majored in electrical engineering, but it turned out my favorite class was the department's weekly entrepreneurship session. Every Friday afternoon, Silicon Valley luminaries who had launched amazing startups would tell their inspirational stories, and I really wanted to be an entrepreneur like them.

However, I ended up in a more traditional role right out of college, taking a consulting job at Sapient, skipping taking time off between college and a first job, and heading straight for the office in downtown San Francisco. This turned out to be a lucky decision, as I was one of the last groups of people Sapient recruited before the dot-com bubble burst at the turn of the millennium and job offers started getting rescinded.

Then, after about a year and a half, I lost my job in one of Sapient's waves of layoffs and started looking for companies that seemed exciting. I had heard of this outfit called Google that didn't impress me much at first. I looked at their home page, saw only a search box, and asked, "Where's the news. Where are the sports scores?"

The norm back then was portals such as AltaVista, Excite, and the early Yahoo. They had search engines, but their business model was based on banner advertising. They used content to draw users into clicking on more pages, so they would see more ads. Their search features were almost an afterthought. Google, a search engine first and foremost, looked bare bones in comparison.

However, Google did seem to be on an upward trajectory, and the simplicity of its interface turned out to be one of its biggest assets. Although they were still quite small, much of their staff had gone to Stanford and a lot of their recruiting was done through Stanford channels. They needed someone who spoke Dutch, because they were taking this new thing called AdWords into European markets.

I ended up joining the company and got employee badge 833. That equated roughly to being one of Google's first 500 full-time employees, since contractors and vendors also got badge numbers. My first job had nothing to do with my ability to speak Dutch. It was just reviewing ads that companies in the US had submitted through Google's self-service advertising platform.

Nowadays, most ad reviews are automated, but back then the technology wasn't good enough to do this. Google was very concerned with not letting any dubious ads get through to results pages, especially those of partners like AOL who had started syndicating Google's ads. So, overqualified humans spent their whole day reviewing ads. Yes, I did dream of ads in my sleep back then.

Reviewing ads was tedious, repetitive, and boring work. I and the other new hires were happy to do it, however, because we all wanted a foot in the door at a company that seemed to be going places.

When Google was ready to launch AdWords in Dutch, I translated the whole interface and much of the support material. I also did all Dutch AdWords customer support until we got to around 5,000 customers. I was basically a jack-of-all-trades assigned to handle anything Dutch-related. At this point, all ads and keywords that were submitted still had to be reviewed manually.

Google then opened an office in Dublin, and I hired some people there to take over Dutch ad approvals and email support, which freed up my time to start working more on the product side. This interested me because I had had a small business in college, advertising on GoTo, the original pay-per-click system, buying keywords to sell videos

I would pick up at the local Blockbuster. I made just about enough money doing this to buy more tech equipment.

A light bulb went off in my head one day at a Google headquarters meeting of the Tier 1-Plus support team. AdWords customers were slotted in support groups based on how much they spent. Tier 1-Plus was the top group: customers who were spending $30,000 or more per month with us. Of course, that amount seems absurdly small now, when Booking Holdings, which owns Kayak, OpenTable, and Priceline, is estimated to be spending a billion dollars per quarter on Google Ads.

During the meeting back then, one of the Tier 1-Plus team said, "All our customers are like super affiliates." I realized that if Tier 1-Plus customers were spending a lot of money, they must be making a lot of money. I started buying keywords for car insurance and eBay, and all of a sudden, I was doing huge amounts of advertising and getting on the phone with American Express (AmEx) daily to negotiate higher credit limits so I could keep my ads running. I quickly became a Tier 1-Plus advertiser myself, to the point that I had a dedicated rep on the same team that I worked on at Google.

Back then, AdWords didn't have anything like search-terms reports or even conversion tracking, systems that are critical for helping advertisers buy the right ads at the right price. The only way that I could make sure I'd be able to repay my AmEx bills was to build those systems for myself, so I could guarantee I would make a profit. The tools I built enabled me to figure out which queries to add as keywords, which ones to add as negative keywords, where to bid more, and where to bid less, all based on conversion data.

All this seems crazy nowadays when there are metrics for everything PPC-related. However, there really was a time when customers were buying AdWords without a good way of tracking results. Clearly, there were results, but they were not measured with any degree of precision. Customers knew AdWords grew their businesses, but the exact elements of the account that drove conversions couldn't be pinpointed.

So, I built my own measuring tools and systems. The product team took notice and said, "Oh, that's pretty cool. We think all our advertisers should be able to do what you're doing." Since I already worked at Google, the AdWords team said, "Why don't we bring you in as a consultant on our projects? You can tell us what we should be building from an advertiser's perspective." I took on what became known as the Product Specialist role: the liaison between the AdWords product teams and advertisers.

ADWORDS STARTS GROWING UP

I was trained as an engineer and actually still write Google Ads script code for my current company, Optmyzr, because I enjoy the engineering. However, my interest was always more in entrepreneurship and building businesses. Obviously, getting customers is a critical part of building any business, and I fundamentally connected with the AdWords system—which is about helping companies find new customers and grow—on that basis.

The other connection of AdWords to entrepreneurship was the paradigm shift Google was creating in the advertising industry. Historically, advertising was both expensive and inflexible. Even a small business that wanted to run an ad on the radio or in the newspaper had to have a budget of a couple thousand dollars or more. The file with the ad was due well before it was slated to air, and once submitted, it was costly and difficult to change even if early results seemed to warrant a different approach.

One of the original AdWords benefits was that you could log in whenever you liked and set any budget you wanted. If an advertiser wanted to do a test with $30 for a month, they'd simply set a daily budget of $1. No traditional media ad sales rep would even pick up the phone for that kind of budget.

You could immediately start seeing which ads were

getting clicks. If you had a tracking system on your website, you could see how potential customers progressed through your web pages and how many clicked on a button to request more information. Advertising was becoming lower risk and easier.

The other handicap of traditional advertising was that, once you determined what the ad was going to say, you couldn't change it, even if you figured out another message that would have resonated with your customers better. You'd have to run the exact same ad for several more days because of production timelines. Also, there was no measurability in traditional media. Of course, you could see if your business was growing or not, but you couldn't know exactly which ad or which aspect of your message was driving those phone calls and purchases.

In 2002, AdWords offered more measurability than traditional media, but by today's standards it was pretty laughable. We knew how many clicks were coming from each keyword and each ad, and the average CPC (cost-per-click) for those, but that was the end of the story. There was still a huge disconnect between an advertiser's business goals and the results Google was reporting.

The evolution of machine learning at Google has always been driven by relevance. When people use a search engine, they expect relevant results. Also, they don't want to be bombarded with ads—unless that ad both looks like and is a useful search result. Then people will happily engage with and click on the ad.

In fact, our ads were so relevant that they often weren't perceived as being ads at all. Once I became the AdWords Evangelist, I used to ask a question every time I gave a talk: "Who here has never clicked on a Google ad?" Half the room would raise their hands. I'd respond, "I don't believe it, because I know how much revenue Google is making. I know most of you with your hands raised have clicked on an ad. It's just that you don't know you clicked an ad because it didn't look like an ad. (This was and is true, even though Google always indicates what results are sponsored.) It's not invasive or intrusive. It's not trying to get you to do something you don't want to do. It actually answered the question you asked Google to help you with. It's so relevant it doesn't seem like an ad."

In the early days, before machine learning was introduced, relevance was determined manually by people like me. Reviewing ads, we would look at the keywords, ad text, and landing pages. The job was to figure out if the ad was relevant. Was the scent of the query being preserved? The "scent of the query" is basically the connection among the keywords, the ad text, and the landing page. If someone types "buy rubber duckies online," the ad should take you to a landing page where you can actually buy rubber duckies, as opposed to an online retailer's home page, where rubber duckies are still a click or two away.

This was still a suboptimal approach to determining relevancy. After all, what did I know about the relevance of a keyword like "replacement flange Toto toilet"? I could sort of figure it out, but I'd hardly be able to call myself a plumber.

Over time, the AdWords team realized, "We've got to use the wisdom of the crowds. We have all this data on how users interact with our search results pages, including the ads. We already know if we show this ad for that keyword 100 times, ten users will click on it." That was the clickthrough rate or CTR. Then we could establish metrics and rules, such as: "If any keyword has less than a 0.5 percent CTR, it should be automatically disabled because it has been shown to be irrelevant."

That approach led to another problem, however. If a user typed in a generic keyword like "jobs," it was likely that they were looking for employment and wanted results for a job-search site. However, perhaps one user in a hundred was typing in "jobs" because they were looking for a Steve Jobs biography. Companies selling the biography would get such a low CTR that the keyword was automatically disabled for them, which was clearly wrong and counterproductive. What about searches when someone really was looking for a book about Steve Jobs? We were failing some advertisers.

So, as AdWords progressed, our team knew we could do better. We could develop a scalpel rather than a jackhammer approach. We could say that in a certain situation a keyword is going to perform better or worse than in another situation. We needed to take into account all the factors influencing the search, like what we knew about the user's location, the time of the day, the additional words the user just put into the search box, and their previous searches. "Predicted CTR," later called Quality Score, the original Google Ads machine learning system, was born.

VISION AND REALITY

When Eric Schmidt was Google's CEO, he hosted weekly company-wide TGIF (Thank God It's Friday) meetings with cofounders Larry Page and Sergey Brin. (Nowadays, those meetings are called TGIAF—Thanks God It's Almost Friday—because, with a global workforce, Google had to start holding the meeting on Thursdays, so it could be recorded and shared with all offices before their weekends started.) At one of these, he set forth his vision for the AdWords system: a business should be able to come to Google, tell us their goals, write us a blank check, and then the system would just handle the rest.

Schmidt saw handling campaigns, ad text, keywords, targeting, and bidding as the mechanisms between the starting point of advertisers buying AdWords and the end point of getting new customers and growing their companies. He envisioned those mechanisms in the middle essentially disappearing from our advertisers' user experience.

That vision was put out there long before machine learning was capable of doing any of this. But, over the years, Quality Score (QS) got better and better at predicting which ads would be more relevant to users, prioritizing them based on big data—the massive amounts of data Google collects on searches and users—processed by machine learning algorithms.

This worked really well for everyone. Users would see more ads relevant to the question they asked and would be more likely to click on them. The advertiser would be happier, because if they got a click, it was more likely to be from a customer who was actually having the exact problem the advertiser could help them solve.

This helped level the playing field. Small businesses that were really putting the effort in to create more relevant ads got rewarded with a higher quality score and lower cost-per-click (CPC). There were many situations in which the small or midsize advertiser was beating the

Fortune 500 companies, because they actually took time to understand how QS worked, and the system was rewarding them with cheaper clicks.

Google was benefiting too, since, in ranking ads based on quality scores, they could better monetize the entire search system. It would make more money because, when ads were more relevant, they would get more clicks per search. All three members of the ecosystem—advertisers, customers, and Google—were coming away happy. Historically, QS has been the flagship of the AdWords machine learning system and to this day still is.

AUTOMATING AUCTIONS, BIDDING, AND TARGETING

The next really significant machine learning tool AdWords introduced was automated bidding. Every time a search happens, an auction takes place to determine the rank of the ads on the Google SERPs (search results pages). The higher the bid and relevance, the higher the placement.

A CPC bidding system like this was clearly better for direct-response advertisers than the more traditional cost-per-mille (CPM) system, which charged a flat rate for a thousand ("mille") impressions, no matter if they were clicked on or not. However, there remained a disconnect between what the advertiser really wanted to achieve and how that could be made to happen.

Google's concept was that bids should be based on cost-per-click (CPC). However, what advertisers really care about in lead generation is cost-per-acquisition (CPA); in e-commerce, it's about return on ad spend (ROAS). How much are you paying for a conversion? Are you selling more of your product or service than you are paying Google? The literal bottom line is: are you making a profit on your advertising budget?

Google started putting automations in place to bridge the gap between the CPC bid used in auctions and advertisers' CPA and ROAS goals. In every auction, Google machine learning would determine, on the fly, how much a given advertiser should bid, given a click's likely conversion rate and their desired target CPA or ROAS.

For example, "sneakers" could be one of your keywords. Let's say a user does two searches: one for "cheap sneakers" and another for "Curry 5 Sneakers." Even though both searches contain the word "sneakers," they indicate two very different intentions from the person doing the search. If somebody is looking for the newest Curry sneakers from Under Armour, chances are they're willing to spend $130 on a pair. If they search "cheap sneakers," chances are they are looking for a discount.

Google could now make a more accurate prediction about intent for this user's search. It's less likely Under Armour is going to sell a Curry 5 when the search is "cheap sneakers," so they should place a relatively low cost-per-click bid, since they can't expect as much value to come out of that particular user clicking on their ad. All this, which is calculated through machine learning, helps the advertiser achieve their return on ad spend goals.

The other major breakthrough in AdWords machine learning involved targeting based on what Google calls "broad match keywords." Google found that about 30 percent of all searches done in a ninety-day period were unique, because people get very creative in the way they formulate what they are searching for.

It was becoming very difficult for advertisers to buy all the keywords a user might type in when they were potentially interested in what they were offering. Broad match keywords were all about identifying searches that were closely related, so advertisers didn't have to worry about covering every single variation a user might come up with for Google to show a relevant ad.

Say you are selling Britney Spears music, posters, or concert tickets. There are 457 ways that people misspell Britney Spears. (If you don't believe me, take a look at this Google archive page: https://archive.google.com/jobs/

britney.html.) If you had to figure out all the 457 wrong ways that people spelled it, you'd be spending a very long time figuring out every single keyword. If you had even just a thousand base keywords, you'd have to do permutations of each of the 457 typos, which would give you a list of 457,000 keywords. It gets insanely complicated.

Despite the benefits of having to manage fewer keywords, a lot of advertisers were forgoing broad match keywords in favor of more restrictive match types like exact match and weren't reaping the benefits of machine learning. Google felt advertisers were missing out on a lot of opportunity and, in 2014 introduced a new solution, "close variants." Regardless of match type, certain keyword variations—misspellings, plurals, singulars, inclusion of function words like "of" and "in"—became treated as if they were the same keyword. Machine learning could figure out which variations were actually close enough to the user's intent in a search that it still made sense to show the ad, even though the search term wasn't an exact match with the keyword.

Close variants made it easier for advertisers to cover the many permutations of keywords a user might type in the query box when searching for essentially the same results. There was a downside to this as well, however, because it took away a measure of advertiser control over how precisely a search term had to match a designated keyword.

Then, in September 2018, Google made one more change to "close variants"—changing its definition of the term—that many in the PPC industry feel went too far. Close variants now meant not only singulars, plurals, and function words, but words that have the "same meaning." This is really only possible with machine learning, because only a "smart" system can figure out, for instance, that "campground" and "campsite," which are not true synonyms, are often used synonymously. All of this has to do with the system's being able to distinguish patterns and similarities in user behavior when one or the other of these words is used.

However, the system was now getting into dangerous territory. Exact-match keywords, which had previously provided a way for advertisers to tell Google to show ads only for queries that were linguistically almost exactly the same, would now allow ads with "similar intent" to the query to be shown. People in the industry felt they had now lost an important level of control. Google no longer respected their instructions, causing anger and angst.

This angst is illustrated in some of the suggested new names for "exact match" in a poll Ginny Marvin ran in Search Engine Land. While the top vote went to "exactish match," there were other submissions like "happy-share-holder match," alluding to the fact the changes helped Google bring in more ad revenue. (See: https://

searchengineland.com/exact-match-our-contest-to-rename-it-for-google-is-sealed-with-an-ish-309092.)

While I am a fan of deploying technology to solve hard problems, like showing ads for searches without having to think of every possible way a user could enter a search term's synonyms, expert PPC strategies depend on being able to control and override automation as necessary. Once again, and as we'll explore more in-depth below, the best results happen when machines and humans work together.

The fact remains that supposed "close variants" are not really synonyms. Sophisticated advertisers may well have figured out slight performance differences in the responses to "campground" and "campsite" that different bids should be able to handle. Google took the ability to make such decisions away from their advertiser customers, who find this very frustrating.

To take another example, say your keyword is "Xbox video games" and someone searches on "video games." Google's machine learning might determine that the match was close and relevant enough to show your ad. That's well and good if you are an advertiser who sells all kinds of video games, but it's quite bad if you only sell Xbox video games. If someone searches on "video games," how do you know they're not looking for Nintendo video games or PlayStation video games? That was frustrating to advertisers who felt they had clearly indicated what they sold and when they wanted their ads to appear, but then the machine learning system came in and overrode those instructions, showing their ad for a more generic variation of their keyword.

True, the machine learning system would eventually figure out if they were showing the wrong ads for a merchant who didn't sell a certain type of video game. The ads would stop appearing because the clickthrough rate would go down when people noticed the ad was actually not that relevant.

Although the problem would eventually fix itself, this was still placing a big burden on the advertiser. If the advertiser's ad text was relatively generic, people would still click on the ad. Only after the click would the user realize the ad wasn't relevant, but now the advertiser had paid Google for a click that wasn't going to lead to a conversion.

Luckily, there are ways to use Google Ads Scripts to counteract some of these more contentious changes in the Google Ads system. This is one of the reasons humans remain so important in PPC. You can figure out tricks and workarounds that will allow you to take back control. An example of such a script is one that automatically identifies when Google is allowing close variants considered as exact matches, and automatically turns those close variants into negative keywords. These workarounds create opportunities for you to do what you feel is best for your clients.

This is an example of humans and machines collaborating to deliver better results. First, the human defines the core keywords for targeting ads. Next, the machine finds additional queries that are relevant to the advertiser's offering. Finally, to prevent waste, the human periodically monitors the machine's work by reviewing search terms reports and adding negative keywords where needed.

Google is happy because they've made PPC advertising easier and better on the average, but nobody cares about averages, especially if you're the advertiser whose results are below average. However, you, a PPC agency or expert working as a "teacher"—see chapter 7 below—can solve the "video games" broad match problem proactively, by installing a script that automatically generates negative keywords when Google machine learning fails to respect the advertiser's actual needs.

WHERE NOW?

Google was now in a position where it had enough data— "big data"—and enough computing power that it could start training machine learning models to pick up on a greater number and variety of patterns and signals. The response has been "Smart"—for "smart," read "machine learning" or "AI"—campaigns.

At the July 2018 Google Marketing Live conference, Google Ads, as AdWords has now been renamed, announced the launch of "Smart Shopping" campaigns, which fully automated targeting, budgeting, and bidding to maximize ROAS (return on ad spend). Google also introduced new ways to prioritize conversion goals, such as valuing new customers differently from existing ones, or valuing foot traffic more highly.

Responsive Search Ads are another recent machine learning innovation. An advertiser can input many different headlines and description lines into the system, and Google Ads then automatically figures out how and when to put these pieces together in response to a specific user query. Before machine leaning got really good, such mix-and-match variations weren't possible.

Google is now acknowledging that online advertising may not be as simple as some people make it out to be. There are still a huge number of businesses that can't and don't do effective online advertising because it involves too many variables. There are too many details to think about, and many businesses don't have the expertise to know what to focus on. A business may not have the time to acquire that expertise and also may not have the budget to work with an agency or consultant. Their DIY approach fails because they forgot to do one of the ten things that really needed to be done.

With the "Smart" initiative, Google is trying to make things easier for these businesses. They can now tell Google, "Here's my goal. Here's what I'm going for, roughly speaking. I'm okay not knowing a lot of the detail and not being able to micromanage everything."

There are two reasons why CPC agencies and consultants are worried about this. First, some clients who have just started to hear the term "Smart" are wondering, "Is this actually going to create a more effective ad campaign than a human agency will?" Clients might get rid of their agencies and the associated costs, believing they are now unnecessary. In theory, smart solutions don't cost anything, as Google still charges on a per-click basis. If you go to an agency, it's not uncommon to pay a 10 percent management fee on top of your ad spend.

The other issue is uncertainty about how quickly artificial intelligence is going to progress. While Smart systems might be pretty good today, it's possible they will really blow your socks off in a year and a half. Unknowns cause fears. That's why it's important to learn something about what machine learning or artificial intelligence really is and what it will actually be able—and not able—to do.

POSTSCRIPT

This is a book about AI and PPC advertising, not about me. But since Google is still the greatest force in PPC advertising, I thought, before getting more deeply into an analysis of AI and its current and future impact, I might say a few words about my "life after Google."

I was a Google Product Specialist and then AdWords Evangelist. I traveled the world and taught people how to take advantage of these amazing advertising systems. I loved the job and its human element.

In the ten years I was at Google, it grew from less than 500 employees to over 60,000. Once a company gets to a certain size, it focuses on scalability. My next logical role was to "train the trainers," staying at the home office and teaching other people to do what I had been doing.

Given my entrepreneurial streak, I decided to leave and start consulting instead. My first client was Google, which hired me back as a consultant to do the job I had done previously, speaking at conferences and teaching people how to use AdWords. I also started picking up other clients who wanted me to manage their accounts for them, and that was an eye-opener.

I knew AdWords was a great product, but real-life account management was still far from streamlined. There were vendors selling products to fix this problem, but they were charging a percentage of ad spend to do so. I couldn't see where my livelihood was if I was charging my client 10 percent and giving half of that to vendors, many of whose tools lacked the features I wanted.

Google had just launched AdWords Scripts, a form of JavaScript that could be inserted in the ad management system to do such things as review accounts as often as once an hour, and seamlessly change bids, pause campaigns, generate reports, and so on. Taking on the "teacher" role, which we'll be exploring below, I started to teach the system by writing scripts to automate some of the things I used to have to do repetitively to keep accounts healthy. This saved a lot of time and money. I met my Optmyzr cofounders through a blog post I did on Search Engine Land about this approach, and suddenly, they and I were full-fledged entrepreneurs in the PPC space.

MACHINE LEARNING BASICS

For most marketing professionals, AI and how it's going to affect PPC advertising are a bit of a black box, and black boxes are scary. The wrong reaction is to pretend AI is just today's buzzword and won't be important tomorrow, so that it's not really anything to be concerned about.

Please understand that artificial intelligence and machine learning are far more than buzzwords. This is something that PPC professionals need to know about, which means obtaining a basic understanding of the technology and its potential. This does *not* require in-depth technical training. You do *not* need to understand the details of how an internal combustion engine works to drive a car, but you *do* need to learn how to operate a car if you want to get around like everyone else.

In computer science, the concept of artificial intelligence has been around since the 1950s. At that time, it also started seeping into popular culture, largely through science fiction. Now, the promise of AI appears to have become a reality and is popping up everywhere, both in the media and in business.

MOORE'S LAW

The current machine learning explosion is the result of Moore's Law, the famous principle that states that computing power doubles roughly every eighteen months. Another way of looking at this is that the size of transistors and circuit boards dropped by half—which leads to a doubling of speed—every year and a half for decades.

Most people have heard of Moore's Law, but it's hard to grasp its real implications, so let's imagine for a moment that Moore's Law applied to the evolution of the automobile. The first car ever made, the Mercedes Benz Daimler, had a maximum speed of about ten miles an hour. In the first year and a half after its invention, you could basically use the car to go across town—ten miles—in about an hour. Eighteen months later, it would go twenty miles an hour, so it would probably now take about an hour to drive from your town to the next in your Benz. Then it doubled again, and you could now do day trips within your state or, if you lived in Europe, drive into a neighboring country.

None of this seems all that dramatic. However, let's say we were able to go through twenty-seven cycles of doubling the car's speed: the same number of times Moore's Law has been in effect since the original inception of AI. All of a sudden, you're talking about going to the sun and back nine times in the hour it formerly took you just to drive across town. In the next iteration of the cycle, you'd be able to take hour-long round trips to the distant planets in the solar system.

The automobile analogy breaks down here, because Moore's law applies to solid-state computing power, not to ground transportation. Thanks to the exponential nature of Moore's Law, the amount of progress in machine learning we're now seeing in an eighteen-month cycle is just mind-boggling, and that's why it's so important to get a grasp on what's happening.

Google's Smart bidding may be pretty good at the moment, but the amount of progress that will probably be made in just the next eighteen months is going to be beyond what we can now comprehend on many levels. We have to be ready for some amazing things to come out of the cycle. There already are many things, and there will be a great many more, that a machine learning system will be able to do better than a human.

PPC MACHINE LEARNING MODELS

Let's return to an examination of the black box. What is and isn't AI? In the media and movies, AI systems are often portrayed as humanoid robots that can basically do anything you and I can do, but much faster and better. In 2016, a major AI breakthrough occurred, in which Google's AlphaGo machine was first able to beat Lee Sedol, world champion at the Asian board game of Go. This was a much more complicated problem than beating a grand master at chess, which occurred in 1997, when IBM's Big Blue beat grand master Garry Kasparov for the first time. Many claim that AlphaGo's victory was the beginning of a "fourth industrial revolution," an AI or machine learning revolution following those of steam, electricity, and the internet.

However, it's important to realize that the practical applications of artificial intelligence in PPC tend to focus on very specific solutions to specific problems that are usually highly structured. Google Ads uses machine learning to figure out the best bid in a certain situation depending, for instance, on time of day, the keywords in a search, and the location of the person doing the search. This involves a lot of statistics, math, and pattern recognition.

AI'S POWER IS EATING YOUR AGENCY: IS IT TIME TO PANIC?

It's been almost eight years since Marc Andreessen told us that "software is eating the world."

Now AI (and machine learning) are eating software.

But is it all just hype?

Is AI really going to replace all those jobs? Why is it "the new electricity"? Is "this time" really going to be different? And most importantly, what are you, as a PPC professional or agency, going to do about it?

I believe you should embrace the changes that are coming. Here's why.

AI is essentially about prediction.

And as the cost, quality, and speed of prediction increase exponentially, the value of human judgment will rise.

What work and tasks are you doing in your agency right now?

I'll bet much of it is based on prediction: predicting the right bid for that keyword or predicting the right targeting to use for a campaign.

How much of that work is focused on creativity? Or strategy? Or cocreating with your clients, not just for them?

Yes, this requires a change of focus for many agencies. Yes, that's going to be difficult. But sorry, get used to changing, or get left behind.

The rate of change in our world today is the SLOWEST

it's ever going to be again. It only increases from here. Ray Kurzweil believes we won't see one hundred years' worth of change in the twenty-first century. Based on today's rate, it'll be more like 20,000 years' worth!

So, get used to reinventing yourself. Please don't play victim.

Embrace what *could be*.

Decide what you want your agency to BE and DO in this new world. Commit to it.

Then, the hard part, have the courage to make the changes needed.

As you build new skills, your confidence will grow. Spoiler alert: it won't be there at the beginning. Sorry, it doesn't work that way.

Surround yourself with a great community (this is why I built AgencySavvy.com) and embrace "failing," because you won't get it all right.

Keep on learning and following smart people like Fred.

And prepare for a wild ride!

MIKE RHODES
FOUNDER, AGENCYSAVVY

While artificial intelligence is a cooler buzzword, machine learning better describes the technology's practical applications to PPC marketing and other business problems. Before it can start making decisions, the system needs to be trained. This is done by using historical data—such as what searches people have done and what links they have clicked on—as input. This input consists of structured and labeled data: data that has been clearly defined and classified, sometimes by human data analysts, often by the characteristics of the database of which it is part.

What you are basically asking the machine learning system is whether it can figure out if the elements of the data set you have input have meaningful correlations with or impact on one another. What are the commonalities and how can these be leveraged? Since the system is being trained with historical data describing real past events, it can then check its output or "predictions" against what actually happened. If there is a discrepancy, the machine learning model being trained is adjusted or tweaked until it is able to give increasingly accurate predictions.

Only after the machine learning model is trained can you input current, real-time data and ask for a prediction. Say you have added a new keyword to your account. When a user searches on this keyword, the system can now make a prediction based on what it has learned so far. A prediction is then generated, a real-time response to such typical PPC questions such as "which of these ads should I show?" or "how much should I bid?"

The system can improve its predictions based on what then happens. Have more users who were presented with this ad clicked on it? If so, the prediction is reinforced.

If not, the system will make adjustments until it yields better results. The process has become a feedback loop largely independent of human control.

Before moving forward to a somewhat deeper look at PPC machine learning models, let's take a step back to programming basics. In simple terms, a computer program takes data as input into the system, processes it according to the code written by its developers, and outputs a result, such as a prediction.

For instance, you could write a simple, intelligent-seeming PPC program that says, "If the keyword is flowers and the user searches for roses, then show the ad. If the keyword isn't flowers, don't show the ad." It's as simple as an "if this, then that" setup. You could say any computer program, however simple, that takes relevant conditions into account and yields a result similar to what a human would have decided, exhibits a form of "intelligence": it is artificially intelligent, in however limited a sense.

This basic approach, however, soon comes up against limitations, like those due to combinatorial explosion, when the number of possible combinations simply gets too large for even the fastest computer to process. As previously mentioned, AlphaGo is generally considered a breakthrough in machine learning and artificial intelligence. There are more permutations of the way the game pieces can be placed on a Go board (~2 followed by 170 zeroes) than there are atoms in the universe (~1 followed by 80 zeroes). It is no longer possible to return results—what should my next move be, and the one after that, and the one after that?—by figuring out every "if-then" possibility, because there are far too many. A completely different approach is needed, and that's where machine learning comes in.

The system now analyzes what is going on at a higher level. What are commonalities of good Go moves? The process is no longer about making an absolutely perfect, 100 percent accurate decision or prediction by modeling every possible move. It's finding a signal in the noise of the plethora of possibilities—the huge number of potential combinations—that need to be considered.

Let's return to the less extreme but still complex example of Quality Score. The goal of QS is to predict an ad's likely clickthrough rate (CTR): whether a user would be likely, when presented with a certain ad under certain circumstances, to click on it. However, the circumstances or conditions under which someone might, for instance, be searching for flowers to buy, can multiply indefinitely, to the point where simple "if-then" logic is no longer capable of taking every critical factor into account.

Google employees known as "raters" rate the relevance of a keyword, ad text, and landing page on a scale of one to five, which helps Google know which algorithms to update to deliver more relevant results in paid or organic results. These ratings are also used by the QS team to find out if there are areas of problematic relevance, entire categories of ads that get low ratings. If so, a machine learning model is created to try to identify future cases of similarly bad ads, and automatically weed them out.

If machine learning models for finding bad ads had too many false positives—flagging a good ad as a bad one—the Google Ads team would go back to the engineers and ask them to adjust the model. They kept doing this until a good balance was achieved, remembering that absolute 100 percent prediction accuracy was not possible.

A good balance meant false positives were at a minimum. After all, it's bad for business to limit ads from good advertisers. Perhaps the model may have erred on the side of including some false negatives—bad ads that were erroneously classified as good ones—so we weren't punishing advertisers by being too strict. However, we didn't want to have too many false negatives either, because that would have meant a bad end-user experience.

The human "rater" process, combined with data from the wisdom-of-the-crowds approach—looking at which ads get the best clickthrough rates—generated huge data sets about what distinguishes good keywords, ad text, and landing pages from bad ones. At this point, PPC machine learning models could start to take the human "raters" out of the process by predicting which newly submitted ads were going to be good, and which bad.

What aspects of machine learning models made this possible? A model can be thought of as a mathematical way to represent the real world. A machine learning model looks for commonalities in huge sets of "real-world" data, such as what makes for a good PPC ad and what makes for a bad one: no simple task. When achieved, models help Google improve the quality of the ads it shows to users. Google makes more money from its ads, and this makes it inevitable that machine learning systems that determine Quality Score will remain a key part of their ads system.

PPC APPLICATIONS OF MACHINE LEARNING MODELS

There are many approaches to building machine learning models, with more being created all the time. The problem becomes identifying which model or models can sort out the commonalities among good and bad PPC ads, a challenge given there are literally billions of new ads submitted to the Google Ads system every year. If an existing model doesn't solve a specific problem, then computer scientists must create one. This doesn't just happen by magic.

The initial goal is to adopt an existing or build a new machine learning model and then train it to the point you have a fairly high level of confidence in the predictions it makes when processing masses of data. Over time and with the input of more data and different scenarios, the confidence level can become higher.

PPC advertising generates huge amounts of data consisting of the answers to such common questions as, "Did somebody buy something from us? If so, how much did they buy? How good was the quality of the lead?" All this can be correlated to other known factors, such as, "What cities do the customers live in? What was the weather in those cities that day? What keywords did they search on?" And so on and so forth.

PPC machine learning models focus on the factors that drive a desired outcome such as conversions. For example, if, after the data is input, the system predicts a higher conversion rate than you originally expected, you—or the system—would probably say, "We now want to bid more in these situations, because there is a higher chance that showing this ad will lead to the desired outcome: a sale." The higher bid will be rewarded by better placement. And, if the machine learning model was correct, improved return on investment.

PPC machine learning models sort through vast amounts of data—far more than human analysts could absorb—to deliver actionable predictions. The results of the predictions then become data input into the system in a feedback loop capable of continuously improving the model's accuracy across a wider set of real-world scenarios and variables.

PPC MACHINE LEARNING NOW

Nevertheless, machine learning took a long time to become really viable in PPC advertising. Ten years ago, when we first started doing this, the process was painfully slow. In the early AdWords days, getting a model developed to a point where its predictions were accurate could take weeks. We had to let systems process massive amounts of data about past user interactions with ads to find correlations that could predict specific behaviors, such as CTR.

Google had massive computing power even in the early days, but most of it was applied to search rather than ads. In 2002, I was taken to a secret location for a tour of Google's data center. It was full of gleaming racks holding beautiful custom-built servers with the wiring very neatly done and highly organized. The number of servers Google was able to fit compactly into the racks was mind-boggling. They were so densely packed, they generated so much heat that the fire alarms periodically went off. The alarm system thought the building was so hot it must be on fire.

Then we came to a small area in the data center, a cage ten feet by ten, that was just a mess. There were off-the-shelf Dell servers, most with blinking red and yellow warning lights. Cables were all over the place. I asked, "What part of Google is this?" The response was, "That's AdWords." Now I understood why AdWords was often really slow and went down frequently. Clearly, much less engineering had gone into the AdWords infrastructure than into search.

There were a lot of uphill battles in the beginning, because Google had this amazing technology, but it wasn't always available to AdWords. This changed, however, when the company began to see that ads were the lifeblood of the business.

Even though AdWords technology had improved, it still took us weeks to build a model, partly because of the sheer quantity of data available. We were a few cycles earlier in Moore's Law, and computing power was more limited. If, at any point during the process, we found we hadn't fed the system the right data or something in the model hadn't been built correctly, we would have to go back to square one and wait another couple of weeks for a new model to be trained. Nowadays, thanks to Moore's Law, new machine learning models are trained in less than a day.

Despite the progress that's been made, it's still important to have reasonable expectations about what automation can do for you, or you will set yourself up for painful mistakes. The truth is that Google's Smart campaigns are not really at the point where Eric Schmidt's vision of handing Google the keys to your bank account and walking away has been achieved.

Actually, you could probably now hand over the keys to your bank account and walk away if all you wanted for your campaigns was average performance. But since you're reading this book, you probably aspire to better results. After all, you know that your boss—whether that's your agency's client or your company's CEO—will be happier having you on their payroll if you deliver the above-average results worthy of a PPC rockstar like yourself. If you want to optimize your PPC campaigns, you still need to define goals, test strategies, monitor results, and intervene as necessary.

The problems PPC advertisers face are simpler than those

faced by companies trying to build self-driving cars—one of my favorite analogies, to which we'll return—where a wrong prediction could prove fatal. Also, the machine learning behind self-driving cars works with data, such as the visual input from a camera, that isn't labeled and structured, meaning that the models involved have to be much more complex.

Granted, things are becoming somewhat more complex in PPC as well, because, for instance, more searches are now based on spoken rather than written input. If you don't want to deal with the "natural language processing" issues this raises—and you probably don't—I believe the Google Assistant and Amazon's Alexa will continue to do a great job on behalf of their advertisers, figuring out how to best understand what users are asking. Then you can simply continue to focus on choosing the right keywords, regardless of whether those will be typed in as queries or asked verbally. Those are jobs you can and should leave to reliable companies with much deeper pockets than your own.

While you don't need to understand such technical details, you *do* need to understand what the Smart system is doing and, just as importantly, *not* doing. Smart Bidding looks at certain factors related to an auction and then sets the bid based on expected conversion rates or the expected value of a click. However, the system may very well not be considering one or more factors that are critical to your particular business, such as specific budgetary constraints or current trends in your industry.

Google Ads isn't the only company applying AI to PPC. There are many different machine learning systems out there that operate independently of one another. Let's look at something relatively simple, like automated bid management. Google gives you one solution, which they call Smart Bidding, but you can also get automated bidding from a plethora of third-party companies that do it differently and, they claim, better. Perhaps one of these takes your industry's usual constraints or other especially relevant factors more fully into account.

Someone needs to figure out which system might be the best solution, given what you know about your clients, based on their industry and the amount of data they have access to. Are you going to experiment with multiple systems? How then do you measure success? Are the two systems you're experimenting with really interoperable?

There is no humanoid robot to sit down at your desk that will figure out everything from bidding to budget to targeting. A lot of human involvement remains: you still have to worry about details like how systems interact, what limitations you need to overcome, and such marketing essentials as to how to position your company's offers to its prospective customers.

Despite their efforts at transparency, Google Ads machine learning remains something of a black box. By black box, I mean that you may not be able to tell if the system is taking a certain factor, such as snowfall levels, into account when it places an automatic bid. That's not at all important in most cases—which is why it may not already be built into the system—but it's very important if you are selling ski resort passes.

That's why you need to understand these technologies on a business rather than technical level. Is the machine learning model overlooking something that is a big driver for your sales? By all means, continue to use Google Smart Bidding, but realize that only you can determine if you need to tweak the system to consider missing factors or data points that can mean the difference between success and failure, or, just as importantly, between average and optimized performance.

PCC professionals continue to play critical roles in all of this. Let's look a little more closely at a ski resort client to see what PPC professionals do better than machines—as powerful and helpful as machine learning can be.

WHAT YOU DO BETTER THAN MACHINES

A ski resort lets Google Ads handle bids for its campaign. The problem is Google Smart Bidding didn't take into account a factor that critically affects today's sales of lift tickets, namely: how much snow fell the previous night!

Data isn't everything and is sometimes unavailable, while human intuition and creativity are inimitable and the best use of a marketing professional's time and abilities. With the ski resort example, it's possible machine learning will pick up on the fact that snowfall matters to your or your client's business...or not. The problem you face as a marketer is that you are relying on a third-party machine learning system that leaves you guessing whether the factors you know matter are being considered and given their proper weight.

WHAT'S IMPORTANT?

If a machine learning model has never looked at a specific factor or data point, such as snowfall levels, then it's just not going to take it into consideration when setting bid levels at auctions. Yes, a lot of amazing things are being done with machine learning. However, in this case, humans didn't train the machine to take a critical factor into account, so you're getting subpar results.

One of your roles as a PPC professional is to teach the machine to look at these factors. You are not going to get the results you want until you have taught the machine what to consider. Once you have, you can let the automation go to town.

There's also the issue of intuitive knowledge, another human rather than mechanical ability. If you ask your GPS, which may not be connected to the web, to give you driving directions, it's basically going to consider all the various routes that you could take between two points. However, it's also going to take some mental shortcuts, make some assumptions or guesses, and look at heuristics and rules of thumb. For instance, it will assume it will be faster to take a freeway than a local road and might not even consider the "surface streets" option. However, you, the driver, might know that there's a new bridge going up on the freeway, which has recently been narrowed from five lanes to three, creating a horrendous bottleneck. Local streets are going to take you to your destination faster than the freeway.

You are the local, not your GPS system, and human intuition is based on such specifics. You live in and know a lot about the area you are driving through, and the machine learning model is probably not considering everything you know. If a change in what it knows has occurred, it may need more time than you do to learn about and take account of it.

THE CREATIVE

While PPC is rooted deeply in data and transactions, compelling creative is still essential for effective PPC advertising. Humans are still better than machines at figuring out and coming up with messaging that is going to resonate and connect with the target audience. That's fundamentally what marketing is: communicating your value proposition to another human being.

The machine might be able to put together a message with phrasing and terminology with some appeal. It does so, however, on the basis of historical data. How have people communicated such information in the past? The system analyzes that data to make an extrapolated prediction. Yet machines have yet to understand emotional connections—how people engage with words and images.

The system hasn't yet seen examples of new types of data that may be especially relevant to the case at hand. It's not good either at encountering or coming up with something entirely new. When new information enters the picture, it is probably sparse in comparison to historical data, and the machine learning system's tendency will be to discount the relevance of this new data. Humans, however, are quite good at distinguishing what is both new or uncommon and important.

People make mistakes and those accidents can become the material of new and often very effective creative approaches. One good example is a Facebook video ad where there was some accidental jittering in a few frames. What was meant to be a static image moved, and the results of the ad with movement were better than those with a static image. This is an example of how evolution can grow out of mistakes. By accident, somebody discovered that adding a tiny bit of motion to a static image was going to draw more attention, get more clicks, and draw more customers in.

A machine learning system might at some point "decide"

to do something novel like add a tiny bit of movement to a static image, but for the most part, this is going to be the result of human intervention. It's people who bring the creative component to advertising, saying, "Hey, let's try a new test. Let's see what happens if we do X, Y, or Z."

SETTING GOALS

When you work with clients, either as an external agency or as part of an in-house marketing team, you have to understand what their business is trying to achieve. Somewhat surprisingly, what a business really wants to achieve with online ads is not always clear to its leadership team. Is the goal to maximize revenue or profit? If the latter, it may mean the goal may be to sell less but at a higher margin. People are better than machines at having focused business conversations with stakeholders and translating what may, in some cases, be confused or convoluted thinking into something that's clear and can furnish the machine with the precise input it needs.

It used to surprise me, when talking to certain Optmyzr customers, that they didn't know they were using Google Ads automated bidding. "How did that happen?" they asked. "I never asked Google to do that."

What often happened is that the advertiser checked off boxes for certain options during campaign setup semi-automatically, without being aware of their choices' implications. The system of course assumed that they wanted the options they selected and turned the features on. There was nothing underhanded here. However, the implications of the choices they were making weren't entirely clear on the surface.

A human PPC professional would have been much better at helping the advertiser navigate such options. A conversation, for example, about the nuances of choosing among the eight different "goal" options on a setup screen would have prevented surprises and problems from arising in the first place.

Even if a customer has consciously chosen Google Smart Bidding, you, as a PPC professional, have to tell the machine what to focus on if it is to do its job properly. Is your goal to maximize conversions, revenue, or new customers? Is it to drive foot traffic to your client's physical stores? What attribution model will you use to best represent your business to the system that sets your bids?

Once you've translated your client's needs into system input, there's the question of how milestones and goals will be measured. You need to decide how to track your metrics. What system might need to be put in place, for instance, to track the number of people coming into your client's stores? While machine learning is great at making calculations, it's you who must tell the system how to obtain the most accurate data needed to make the best possible predictions or decisions.

What needs to be measured is not necessarily simple. A "conversion" involves many different steps, so it's useful to think in terms of micro-conversions as well as the macro-conversion or actual sale. You'll have more micro-conversions—the smaller steps on the path, including prospective customers signing up for an email list, visiting a landing page, or reaching out for more information than macro-conversions.

Here's a graphic illustrating the difference between micro- and macro-conversions. The size of the bubble represents how much value each type of conversion delivers to your business.

MICRO AND MACRO CONVERSIONS

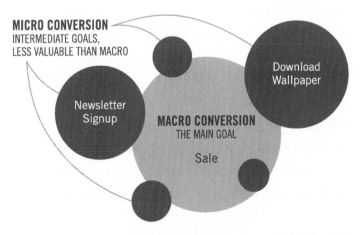

MICRO CONVERSION
INTERMEDIATE GOALS, LESS VALUABLE THAN MACRO

Newsletter Signup

Download Wallpaper

MACRO CONVERSION
THE MAIN GOAL

Sale

Here's a related graphic illustrating the importance of micro-conversions. It shows that in most cases, there is more data about the less important conversions.

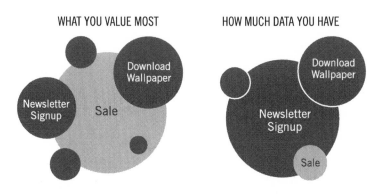

WHY MICRO CONVERSIONS ARE IMPORTANT
Micro conversions give you more data for optimization

WHAT YOU VALUE MOST

HOW MUCH DATA YOU HAVE

Download Wallpaper

Newsletter Signup

Sale

Download Wallpaper

Newsletter Signup

Sale

SETTING TARGETS

You may be working with a law firm that only wants to spend $2,000 per month for online advertising. You know that clicks for legal ads are some of the most expensive in the business, so you're not going to get a lot of macro-conversions or actual sales with that kind of budget. You may also have to struggle with Google Smart Bidding's criteria. For instance, it may not do automated bidding for a certain campaign if you don't have at least fifteen conversions per month. Struggle though you might, you're unable to hit that minimum with such a limited budget. Now your only option is manual bid management and to wait until you get to a high enough number of conversions to start using Smart Bidding.

However, as a PPC professional, you could do a bit of thinking and say to your client, "Okay, we're having a hard time getting fifteen new clients every month, but we do get a hundred people downloading your whitepaper on mesothelioma. We also know that after you email these people three or four times, they are much more likely to contact you for a consultation and turn into clients. So why don't we track whitepaper downloads as micro-conversions and maybe optimize against that?" When data is sparse, as it often is, it's up to you, not the machine, to figure out the desirable preliminary steps other people go through before reaching a decision and to set those as "conversions" that the automated system can then use to make decisions.

Machine learning works really well with finding patterns in data, especially large amounts of or "big" data. Big data was a buzzword a while back and remains a reality. It's only because we are now able to collect massive amounts of data through global online systems such as Google or Facebook that machine learning systems are viable. The system needs to be able to process a tremendous amount of historical data and examples to find meaningful signals in the noise. That's why Google is in such a great position. They basically see the data from every historical scenario, including outcomes, where a user was presented with and clicked on an ad. Machine learning makes data more useful because of its amazing ability to find hidden correlations that can turn big data into big payoffs by finding smart insights.

Let's say you have one client—the law firm—who spends a couple thousand dollars a month on PPC and another client—perhaps a ski equipment manufacturing firm— that spends a half million dollars a month. In either case, the client still has far less access to data than Google has. The question in both cases is: what data and factors are truly important to the client's business goals? Time of day? User location? Snowfall levels?

If a machine learning system is trained with either too few or too many variables, results can become skewed and the factors that really count not given proper consideration. You, however, have developed human intuition about what's important, because you have worked on this type of problem before and have seen how a business grows and achieves its goals based on certain specific factors. You don't sit on this experience and wait for the machine to pick up on it somehow. Using your intuition, you can get the ball rolling in the right direction. The system will continue to learn along the way, yielding more and better results, but you and your professional experience can accelerate the process, particularly in the beginning.

MEASURING AND REPORTING RESULTS

Back in the early AdWords days, those of us on the Google Ads team felt that marketing was too often driven by the HIPPO: the highest paid person's opinion. We were convinced that was the wrong way to go about making marketing decisions. To help change that, Wesley Chan, an early product manager at Google, formed a team that acquired a small San Diego company, Urchin, in 2005. Before the acquisition, I flew with Wesley to San Diego to meet the team, and when the deal was done, I helped transition Urchin's support operations to Google. Urchin became the nucleus of what is now known as Google Analytics.

Paul Muret, Jack Ancone, and brothers Brett and Scott Crosby, Urchin's founders, knew that decisions shouldn't be driven purely by gut instinct: certainly not when you have enough data—such as on what users do when they come to your site after clicking an ad—to make truly data-driven decisions. However, especially in any campaign's initial phase, you may not have enough data to tell a story that has actual statistical significance. Even when you do, it's still not the HIPPO that should be driving the final decision. You and your client are sure to have institutional knowledge that can point you in the right direction. As a marketer, you have previous experience with similar clients in this same vertical.

Machine learning systems provide a great basis for doing A/B ad testing to determine if one or two alternatives is a winner and the other a loser. Very often, however, there is neither an undisputed winner or loser, possibly because there simply wasn't enough relevant data at the time of the test to make a clear determination. In that case, the test results are often just put on a shelf.

A better approach is to get creative and ask, "Well, since these ad tests are too close to call, what might actually distinguish the new ad and make it much more effective?" If some time has passed, there might also well be enough new data to enable the system to make a clearer prediction using the first or another A/B test.

Similarly, tools such as Optmyzr are great at generating reports with metrics and KPIs. However, defining the targets and picking the most useful KPIs to help meet those targets are where human knowledge and intuition still beat machines. PPC experts in consultation with their advertiser clients can best determine what data should be considered in order to meet business goals.

MESSAGING THAT CONNECTS

The basic premise of search and, in fact, all marketing, is to connect a business with a consumer who has a specific problem the business is able to solve. Google Ads acts like a matchmaker, matching businesses to consumers with specific needs.

In thinking about PPC machine learning, we often focus on bid management and budget management—all very numbers-driven factors. However, in most cases, your client's business is not going to be the only one providing a solution to the problem it is addressing. Unless your business is unique for some reason, which is unlikely, you are going to be facing a lot of competition.

At this point, one thing that can make you stand out is higher bids, but in the final analysis, that's not going to cut it. Basically, you're saying, "I'm just going to spend more than everyone else. That's going to be the lever growing my business." However, that approach hits the limits of practicality very quickly.

How then do you distinguish yourself as a business offering a solution to a problem similar to those offered by other businesses? It's about your messaging and the human, creative side. What sets you apart is your unique value proposition and call to action. How is your service or solution better than the competition's? Have you been in business longer? Does your product have more features or a lower price point? Do you have a better guarantee? What can you put in the message that's going to draw more people to your ad, whatever your bid might be?

The creative, human element in marketing is how you position your product in a way that makes it desirable and appealing to someone who can choose from a wide variety of alternatives.

We're seeing again, to a greater extent than ever before, that brands really do matter. Amazon is so successful because customers know what it stands for. They know that if you buy something from Amazon Prime, you'll get it in two days. Even if you don't get it in two days for some reason, their customer service will be great at making things right. Given the choice of buying from Amazon or another retailer you haven't previously used, the Amazon brand will matter a lot.

That makes it all the more important for you to help your client's business, which may be competing with Amazon, figure out, "What makes us unique?" Are we working with local vendors? Do we have better prices than Amazon—which at this point is actually no longer the price leader but the convenience leader? What are the opportunities for you to make your offering stand out by connecting through messaging, promotions, or price?

What you as a PPC professional continue to do really well is think of the ad text and images that will be shown on a variety of advertising channels when your prospective customers are ready to be swayed your way. Shopping ads, for instance, are all about promotions. What kind of specials are you offering? What is your pricing strategy? Is there free shipping? Are there bulk discounts? If you do this manually, you're using intuition about "human factors." Or if you employ narrow AI solutions to help answer these questions, you, the human PPC professional, will still play a role in connecting the multitude of narrow AI systems together, so they work in tandem to achieve the desired outcome.

This may seem somewhat obvious and high-level, although that doesn't prevent PPC professionals forgetting it when they hear about Google's latest machine learning initiatives. However, content creation often involves significant subtleties. Remember the jiggling Facebook ad? This was basically a human mistake that led to the discovery that, in some cases, ads that are slightly moving can be more effective than those that are not.

REPETITION AND DIFFERENTIATION

I once did a blog post with David Greenbaum, who was CEO of Boost Media at the time (https://searchengineland.com/3-proven-ways-write-ads-deliver-conversions-209476). Boost was trying to figure out what the elements of the best ad texts were. As an example, you get very different performance if you put "need" rather than "want" into an ad, and vice versa. If you're running a B2B ad, touting the features businesses "need" might perform better, while in a B2C ad, "want" might connect more with the intended buyer. If someone is buying new clothes, most often they don't necessarily need but want a new outfit. However, if you're looking for a plumber, you don't "want" your toilet to be fixed; you "need" it to be fixed.

These are the subtle differences in word usage that can have a dramatic impact. Machine learning doesn't yet do a very good job at taking linguistic subtleties into account. Whether it will ever be able to do so is an open question, but let's just say that machine learning systems don't speak English to one another every day, as you, your client, and your client's customers do.

While machine learning can analyze variations in meaning and connotation among synonyms or near-synonyms, this is something humans already intuitively know. Nuances also vary from country to country. English in the UK is different in often subtle ways from American English. Although machine learning could master such nuances, human intuition already puts you ahead of the game and in a better position to make the word and other choices that will convey your message best.

Here's an example of the message an ATM in England might display while handling a withdrawal:

Call me oversensitive, but as a Californian using the machine, I found this message somewhat off-putting. An ATM in the United States would probably say something like, "We are *processing* your request." By way of contrast, to an American, the phrase "*dealing with*" sends a subtle but significant signal that the machine feels you are bothering it by making your request, and that it is somewhat annoyed with you.

One project we had at Google was Ad Libs, based on the word game Mad Libs. The Ad Libs system would ask some questions such as: what is your vertical and what is your city? The answer could be: a restaurant in Palo Alto, California. The system would spit out an ad for your restaurant. If you told them what type of cuisine the restaurant featured, the system could also put that into a template.

The problem was that everyone started to use the Ad

Libs system, and all the ads for a search for restaurants in Palo Alto started looking the same. Not only was this a marketing problem, but it also created a technical one. Once every ad starts looking the same, machine learning gets stuck. To continue to evolve, machine learning systems need a variety of inputs and the results of different types of experiments to determine what works and what doesn't.

The more homogeneous the ads became, the more boring customers found them, so they stopped clicking on the ads. Our advertisers began to wonder if there might be a bug in Google AdWords. There was some sort of a bug, although it wasn't a problem with the underlying programming.

The machine learning system was also getting stuck because, if everything that shows up on the page is basically the same, the system can no longer predict what's going to work better or worse. The machine learning model stops "learning" and improving. PPC professionals remain a necessary part of the machine learning process, because they introduce variation and uniqueness and can come up with and try different approaches.

There is a cosmetics company called Younique Products, and, for whatever reason, spelling the word "unique" as "Younique" really resonated with the intended audience.

Its PPC ads had much higher clickthrough and conversion rates than normal. This was a pun based on a variation in spelling, one that a machine would never have come up with. For whatever reason, perhaps a currently popular cultural "meme," the name seemed cool, and the approach worked very well. A funny, odd, or distinctive spelling that may resonate is something a machine will never generate.

ADS AS INFORMATION

One reason AdWords ads became so successful is that users perceived them as information. Google's founders, Larry Page and Sergey Brin, didn't like and didn't want to do advertising. They must be happy they changed their minds, because advertising has made the company they founded one of the most successful in history. The founders only got behind Google AdWords after being told and convinced that "ads can be information, just like the search results that we show."

People use a search engine because they need help. They might have a broken-down car or a backed-up toilet. They might be looking for a new dress. Ads can be thought of as information helping users get what they need or want and are a means of connecting them to the businesses that offer the needed goods and services. If you're a plumber, you want people to pay you to fix their toilets.

Rather than having a search direct them to a web page or YouTube video showing how to fix a toilet, most people would rather find a plumber who can do the job.

Thinking about ads as information is a valuable perspective. This also means that you as a PPC marketer may have to limit your creativity slightly. The moment you start doing too much traditional lifestyle-oriented marketing and not really answering the question someone has asked in the search field, users become more resistant. They start looking at and thinking about the search result as an ad. They feel like they're being marketed to and might decide not to engage with the ad, engaging with the "organic" search results instead.

The Google Ads Smart learning systems have now started to mix and match combinations of text in the ads they display. What are called Responsive Search Ads have already been mentioned. Google is now asking you not to write entire ads but ad components, which the system will decide how to mix together. Nevertheless, the system is still asking you, as a PPC professional, to provide several variations of a headline: some short, some long, some that mention your client's store's name, and some that don't.

What Google Ads is essentially asking is for you to feed the system several variations of "creative" data. However, the machine learning system is not going to figure out what your client's value proposition is or what makes its store special. That's what you need to contribute, because only you know your clients' goals and needs, and how best to create messaging around them. This first stage—how your clients usually promote their businesses; what they typically say about themselves that gets customers to buy—is still up to you. The machine has no clue about all this. Only once you give your input can you let Google do the heavy computational lifting.

MICRO-SEGMENTATION

In many ways, machine learning is making the creative aspect of PPC more interesting than it used to be. A couple of years ago, if you were selling sneakers, AdWords asked you to write two or three ads about them. There was no notion of who the person on the other end of the computer was. Is it a woman? Is it a man? What's their age? What's their household income? Even more importantly, how many times have they visited your site before? When they came to your site was there a specific style of sneaker they looked at?

Now Google has added new ways to target audiences allowing you to show different ads or change bids as appropriate. The challenge becomes that there may now be so many different permutations you can't or don't want to set up an ad group for each possibility. It makes more sense to let machine learning make predictions about CTR and conversion rates, showing the ad that is more likely to lead to a conversion and making the bid that will best help meet an ROAS goal.

Since you can target increasingly focused segments, you now need to create more ad text variations. You need to figure out what ad text might resonate with a female between twenty-four and thirty-five years old who visits your client's website frequently. What do you say to her, as opposed to what you say to the sixty-five-year-old male who has never been to your site before?

In the final analysis, it is no longer just about pitching your product. It's figuring out what the potential customer cares about. To go back to the hotel example, even if users make very similar searches for hotel rooms, it really does matter if you are able to know whether a specific user tends to be a bargain hunter, a luxury traveler, or someone really into local experiences and hotels, as opposed to big chains.

Different things are going to resonate with each type of user. So, rather than writing two or three generic hotel ads, you can now tout some specific benefits, creating many more variations. You might now be looking at dozens or hundreds of different ads being fed into the system, because it can now connect the right ad to the right audience. You as the marketer need to identify the personas, your major target audience segments, and write compelling creative for them. Machine learning can then deploy your work to the right users at the right times.

However, just because you can target smaller and more precisely defined customer segments doesn't mean you should spend time writing ads for them all. Your time is precious, so you, as a smart marketer, should focus on the highest priority segments and leave smaller, less important ones to automation.

A machine learning system won't ask you to write a couple more ads targeting a specific audience segment. It's up to you to figure out who your target audience is. Even big brands like Target need to do this. Everybody shops at Target, but when Target does a marketing campaign, it's directed to one or more personas. Perhaps it has fallen behind in a certain market segment, defined by a specific persona, so there is potential for growth there.

What can you say to a persona to inspire them to come shop at Target? These decisions are still driven by these companies' leadership and marketing teams and have nothing to do with Google Ads machine learning. Once you define your audience persona, it's up to you to find a creative solution for attracting their business. The technology on the back end will help you iterate on and measure tests, as well as manage how the campaign is deployed, but the creative element is still the marketing professional's job.

The same need for focus applies to targeting. Returning to the example above, if you find that the majority of your customers are females aged twenty-five to thirty-four, you probably want to create ad text variations that will resonate with various sub-segments of that audience. You may not want to focus at all on the sixty-five-year-old man who is less likely to buy from your website.

Google Analytics can and will help you figure out who your client's typical customers are, providing the data upon which you can build personas and do targeting. If you're building a remarketing list, for instance, who has visited your client's site before, how many times, and what pages do they typically visit?

TAKING A BROADER VIEW

Thanks to advances in targeting technology, we've come closer to one-to-one online marketing. This may drive better results in terms of ROAS, but it can also negatively impact your brand. Take remarketing: identifying users who have already interacted with your client's website and deciding which ads to show them. When a user comes to a page on your client's site, Google drops a cookie to be able to recognize that same user elsewhere on the internet. If a user came to your page looking for Adidas sneakers, and then does a search for "best running shoes," you might say, "I want to bid more for this customer now, since, because of the research they've done, I know they're further down the path to conversion and more likely to convert soon."

So, you make a higher bid, or the system does so automatically. You can also say, "I don't want to show my generic ad. I want to show a completely different, specific ad that says, 'We've got a 10 percent discount on Adidas right now.'" That offer will really resonate with the user, who was already thinking about buying Adidas running shoes.

As powerful as this is, it can also lead to what many people consider annoying advertising. If you remember what happened to Excite and Lycos, you'll know this is a very big red flag. Having been overly focused on monetizing their sites with annoying banner ads, they went out of business a long time ago.

Remarketing ads can be equally annoying. This is a scenario you've almost certainly encountered as a user. You research a product on one site, and then later, while reading the news on another site, you get incessantly bombarded with display ads with pictures of what you just looked at. If you just let the machine go at it, its only mission is to attain the goal you've given it: to get as many conversions as possible. The machine doesn't know that it's bad to annoy people. It's only been instructed to make sales. The machine will show the ad again and again, because each time it's shown, there's a chance the user might convert. After all, they showed an interest in the product by visiting the product's site earlier.

This is where humans can and must take a broader view. You can say, "Maybe these remarketing ads on display provide cheap clicks with a decent shot at converting, but if users still haven't bought from us after seven days, perhaps we should just give up on it. Let's not bother them and hurt our brand reputation. Let's back off and not creep them out."

There's an extreme example of this that's quite instructive. Someone invented a video game in which you, the player, are running factories that produce paper clips. (See: https://www.wired.com/story/the-way-the-world-ends-not-with-a-bang-but-a-paperclip/.) An optimization problem arises. You get to say how many factories you have running and how many people are working in them. Then artificial intelligence kicks in, and the factories begin optimizing the manufacture of paper clips.

At the end of this game, everybody inevitably dies. The

lesson is that, when you set a business goal and give it to an entity with no compassion and a narrowly defined goal with few constraints, you have forgotten the machine is now tasked with just that one thing. If the machine is tasked with building as many paper clips as possible, it will eventually use up all the world's resources doing so. So, the machine's decisions in its effort to make more paper clips eventually leads to the end of the human race. It doesn't know that it's pointless to produce paper clips when there are no people left to buy them, or that in any event killing people to use their bones to make paper clips is not the right thing to do ethically.

That's one of the problems in machine learning. If you task a machine with just one goal, without context, it will sometimes go too far in a direction you actually don't want it to go. Remarketing is not as morbid or extreme an example as the paper clip game, but it is a good illustration of automation being too narrowly defined and leading to unintended side effects like annoying your prospective customers.

To reemphasize, fully generalized machine intelligence—what people who have seen a lot of science fiction and horror movies think of as "AI"—has not yet arrived. It may never do so in our field. It's only to such generalized AI that you could say, "Here's my business goal. Go at it. Just handle all the advertising for me." The reality is that we have all these specialist machine learning solutions, and we as humans must still decide what to put into play. Which machine learning models work well together, and which might be competing with each other, leading to undesirable results.

OPTIMIZATION AND CONSTRAINTS

Another of your jobs is to figure out if you will use Google's or a third-party's technology. This becomes an optimization problem. The Google technology might be free of charge, but perhaps there's a slightly more expensive third-party technology that produces somewhat better results. Is it worth paying for that? You might want to conduct an experiment to determine which system is better for your needs. Then, when a new client comes along, you can skip a lot of costly experimentation and point the client in what you've already discovered is the right direction.

However, since Google Ads is layering on more and more automation tools, it's becoming more complicated to sort through which ones make the most sense given your clients' industries and goals. Then, there's the related problem of whether you and your client have enough data for the system to work properly. You might see certain bidding-automation tools working really well for high-volume items sold by major retailers. At the same time, you might find the machine is not doing very well with mid- or low-volume items, because it's simply not getting enough data points to discover commonalities and do any meaningful optimization.

The first question is which automation tools, of all those you have access to, work best for your client's needs. The second question is whether the client is big enough to be willing to spend enough money to make these automated processes viable.

The third question involves constraints. There will be problems if you just ask the machine to get as many conversions as possible but don't tell it how much money you can spend. If you say, "Get me as many conversions as possible," does that mean you're willing to spend a million dollars to get a new customer? Probably not, unless you're selling a two-million-dollar race car, and maybe not even then, because the margins would be too low. You must determine what constraints need to be put into play.

Such business constraints are not always as black and white as people like to think. I constantly ask clients, "What's your acceptable cost-per-acquisition for a new lead?" A lot of them just can't tell me. Even if they understand how much a customer is worth to them, the amounts they're at first willing to spend are unreasonable.

The client may need to be reminded that it is not a good idea to forgo logic if you want good results. If I say you need to spend fifty dollars per click for someone who might potentially be a new customer for your client's law firm, that freaks a lot of clients out. They say, "Fifty dollars is a lot of money for just one click!" However, let's say that for every twenty people who click on the law firm's ad, four will fill out their information, and one will become a customer. So, to get one customer, you need twenty clicks at fifty dollars each, which is $1,000. If you know that your client's typical customer is worth $5,000, you know that's a good deal, one you should take.

That's where the human element comes in again. When your client says, "Fifty dollars a click is way too much," you have to reason with them and respond, "Well, listen, it does sound expensive. I understand that it's scary, but historically when we've done this, these are the kinds of conversion rates we see. Remember, you just told me that a customer is worth $5,000, so this is something you should do." If you don't have the human expert who has been through this sort of thing before and can provide a rationale for a high CPC, a client probably won't take the leap of faith and might not get the results you would have been able to deliver.

At the beginning of this chapter, we saw how a human with local knowledge might easily be better than a GPS system at figuring out the fastest way to get from point A to point B. The local has the advantage. In marketing, humans are still the locals. The creative, human factor has not been replaced.

Is the human factor ultimately replaceable? Until recently, I would have said, "No, absolutely not." After the triumph of Google's AlphaGo Zero, I'm starting to wonder a little. That machine learning system was so powerful it no longer needed the data from games played by humans to beat a human Go master. All that's needed is enough computing power to run a huge number of extremely quick simulations. Returning to Moore's Law, that computing power has been attained and will continue to expand.

However, hundreds of millions of dollars were invested in the development of AlphaGo Zero. So, while the human factor may—just may—be replaceable, for now, it can only be replaced at a cost that's much too high to be viable. As you'll see below, it's often far more effective for machine learning systems to collaborate with humans than to replace them.

There are things that humans do and will probably continue to do better than machines. However, tools do bidding better than humans can do it manually. This is one thing that computers, if they have the right input, do better than you.

4

WHAT MACHINES DO BETTER THAN YOU

Susan is an experienced PPC professional, a marketer who started doing bid management in 2003. At that point, AdWords was basically asking, "What is the cost-per-click you are willing to pay if a user clicks on your ad?" Susan set up some advanced campaigns: one directed at California, and another, selling the same product, targeting New York State. She established slightly different bids for each of those campaigns, but the process was all quite manageable.

Then bid adjustments came along. Google began allowing you to modify or adjust bids based on a number of factors: different hours of the day, days of the week, geographical regions, and device types. Now Susan is being asked, for instance, "Do you want to bid the same or a different amount if somebody's searching from Los Altos, California on a mobile device at 7:00 a.m. on a Tuesday? Things are getting too complex for Susan to consider every possible scenario.

EXPONENTIAL COMPLEXIFICATION

This process of complexification has increased exponentially. For time of day, Google Ads allows you to set up six different options. Most advertisers define these options broadly: say from 6:00 to 9:00 a.m., 9:00 a.m. to noon, noon to 3:00 p.m., 3:00 to 6:00 p.m., and so on. However, you can define these options with any level of granularity you wish, down to periods of fifteen minutes. Of course, if you define all six different options in terms of fifteen-minute intervals, you will have covered only ninety minutes of the day in all, which is rarely practical. This is why Optmyzr allows setting up to twenty-four time options, one for each hour of the day.

To time of day, add demographic profiling, including user age and gender, as well as whether the user has been to your site before, and to which pages. The number of segments you can start to look at multiplies rapidly, and bidding is based not on a single but a combination of any number of these segments.

Susan and her clients now need to make an ever-growing number of bids. In fact, even if only one keyword is involved, tens of thousands of bids need to be set, based on every potential factor:

1,000 location * 3 devices * 2 genders * 5 age ranges

= **180,000 *bid permutations*** *for one keyword*

Of course, nobody has only a single keyword. Let's return to 2003. Google asked Susan and other digital marketers for cost-per-click (CPC) bids. However, nobody, aside from Google, really cared about CPC. What businesses cared and still care about is getting new customers and the cost-per-acquisition of those customers. They want to know how much of a profit or return they will make on their ad spend.

Susan and others like her were doing the math on this purely out of necessity. Machine learning had yet to arrive, and the bidding process wasn't yet automated. Susan turned from being a traditional marketer into much more of a spreadsheet junkie, just because, in the PPC environment, she had to become one.

The word "computer," as you know if you've seen the films *The Imitation Game* or the documentary *Top Secret Rosies,* did not originally mean a machine, but one of the women who did computations for the British Secret Service in World War II. "Computer" was a job title.

However, generally, when the IBM mainframe computer came online, "computer" stopped being a job. Eventually, the women doing these calculations were no longer necessary. You stopped using pen and paper to calculate how to put a spaceship on the moon and bring it back. The machine got the answers much more quickly and with far fewer errors.

The same thing has now happened with PPC bid management. Computers are better at it than humans. With the advent of machine learning, we have gotten to a place where you can tell Google your client's business goal, and bids will be adjusted accordingly. You can also start talking about the lifetime value of customers—which we'll return to—and let Google's Smart Bidding figure out the right bid for each of the millions of potential criteria that might lead to a conversion.

This was driven home during one of my early client meetings. Everything had been done over email with clients, but at a certain point, Google decided to do in-person client meetings with some of its advertisers, especially those who were spending significant amounts of money on AdWords.

My team and I went down to San Diego to meet with

an agency. Four people from the agency attended the meeting. We got fifteen minutes into the presentation, and one of them fell asleep. We all looked at each other, as if saying to one another, "What the hell's going on here? We're Google, a company everyone wants to talk to. Advertisers have been asking to meet with us for a long time. Here we are, actually having face-to-face client meetings, and this woman is falling asleep. How weird is that?"

Picking up on our thoughts, the woman's boss, the head of the agency, said, "Please forgive her. She's in charge of making sure the ads are turned on every morning and off every evening. Her job is to come in to the office very early to turn the ads on for the day, and then she's the last one to go home, having made sure the ads are all turned off for the evening."

We couldn't believe it. An actual human being had to push the buttons to enable and pause ads? It made no sense. The poor woman literally couldn't keep her head on straight because she was so tired. We realized that this was a function we could easily automate, so we did.

ATTRIBUTION MANAGEMENT

Automating start/stop times, of course, was just the beginning. Automation became applied not only to dayparting, but to such other critical tasks as bid management and attribution modeling, that is, determining the degree of credit to be given to each of the prior actions leading up to a conversion. Traditionally, advertisers relied on so-called last-click attribution, which means giving all credit to the last event before the conversion, and for years the whole industry was built on this model.

Now we can do better because we have more data and computers fast enough to do advanced modeling. The last-click attribution model was never really good enough, and we can now be more precise. Not only that, but the territory we want to map has become more complex. Ten to fifteen years ago, users who needed something would have maybe ten to twelve online interactions—for instance, do ten to twelves searches—prior to making a purchase. Today, people are all over the place, having hundreds of online interactions. They may be on social networks, watching videos, reading articles, seeing display ads, all while switching between devices like their Google Home Hub, a mobile device, and their work computer. Machine learning can be used to support the math to determine the value of each such complicated interaction in sophisticated models like data-driven attribution models.

If you value only the last click before the sale, you're forgetting about everything that made that last click possible.

Exposure to your client through a social network, a display network, or a YouTube video ought to be counted as well. Machine learning makes a variety of attribution models other than the last-click possible. You could value the first or the last interaction more highly, or you could have a much more complex model giving different weights to any number of interactions leading up to a conversion. This, again, is the type of complex mathematical task that machines do better than humans.

These include data-driven attribution models, which look more closely at individual interactions and connections. Rather than taking only broad-strokes generalizations into account, these models can look at each specific interaction. For example, say a user searches for "sneakers." Then they realize, "Oh, I actually meant running shoes," and do another search on that keyword. Then they realize that they really like a certain brand of running shoes, say Adidas, and search on that.

The user has done three searches and now converts. What Google Ads data-driven attribution can do is look at that middle query and ask, if the user now searches for "running shoes," how much more likely is it that they will eventually convert? Then specific ratings can be assigned. In real time, the system can actually ask and determine, "Based on this user's history, what they are likely going to search for in the future, and the specific search they are making now, what is the probable value of this click in helping the advertiser achieve the end goal?" That goal could be hitting a target return on ad spend, maximizing conversions, maximizing conversion value, or something different.

This is yet another great job for machine learning. It is such a massive data-analysis problem that humans would have almost no clue where to start looking, given that their spreadsheets would now contain millions, even billions, of data points. Machine learning can see signals based on even small correlations and then set better bids, helping the advertiser get more value from what's happening online.

If the woods are really thick, it's hard for us humans to spot a single tree. However, let's not discount humans entirely. If you give statisticians data and ask them to run a regression or other model, they'll probably come up with some answers that will drive more conversions, but it might take them six months to come up with the answer. If your statistician isn't familiar with the specific model that could have found the signal amidst the noise, you are out of luck. The answer you will get six months later will probably have too low a correlation with actual conversions to be useful.

GOOGLE ANALYTICS

The evolution we're seeing now is no longer just about having access to lots of data. It's machine learning systems' ability to figure out the interesting correlations within these huge data sets. Google Analytics is, again, a good example. Back prior to 2002, before AdWords came along, we lived in a "no data" marketing world. You basically spent money on advertising in the hope that it would pay off. You measured if you were succeeding by what was happening to your business's bottom line, but the metrics were far from exact.

With AdWords, now at least you knew how much you were spending on a keyword and how many clicks you were getting from an ad, but you really didn't know what happened after the click. Again, you were basically just hoping that sales would result. If you could tell your business was growing, more or less, you'd assume your PPC ads were probably working.

When we acquired Google Analytics, we told our customers, "Now we're going to track people as they come to your website, and we're going to know exactly what they do." We knew what keyword and click brought the user to your site, and we now also knew what users did on the site, whether they filled in a lead form or bought something.

Now we were able to track and store a tremendous

amount of data—big data—about the thousands, even millions, of clicks that have driven a prospective customer to your client's website and what happened with each of them. Machine learning systems start to see signals in all this data and deliver reports on the results.

Marketing professionals and their clients may ultimately determine what needs to go into these reports and how they should be interpreted. Where Google Analytics excels is in generating these reports by analyzing the relevance of huge amounts of data to your business needs.

At this point, Google Analytics can automatically flag business intelligence. When manually looking at the data, you might notice online conversions were up but have missed that, in fact, in New York conversions have dropped, an anomaly compared to the rest of the account. Thanks to the machine generating this insight, the human can go to work figuring out what happened in NY—perhaps a negative post about your product in a local paper. You had to do a lot of setup to give the system all the data, but now you can get answers to your questions even before you ask them.

ANALYSIS AND PREDICTION

Another of the steps along the way to Google Ads's current machine learning system was the Google Prediction

API (application programming interface), an on-demand service where you could feed data into the system and ask it to build a prediction model. Google would take the data and run it through nearly twenty different statistical models. A typical or average team of statisticians tends to work with the three or four models they already know. If they were to turn to a new model, it would typically take six months to build it out and figure if it worked properly.

The Google prediction API already had seventeen models running and took roughly an hour to come up with an answer as to whether the model had a high correlation or statistical significance. The model could then be used to make ongoing predictions.

Google used this system internally in a creative way that provides a good, concrete example of how machine learning works. As Google got bigger and bigger, a ticketing system was put in place. Any Google employee with a problem could go to the internal website and file a ticket: perhaps to get something fixed, to get a new computer, or if they needed more printing paper.

One time, I saw a raccoon running around the Google campus in broad daylight. I thought to myself that raccoons only run around in broad daylight if they are rabid, so someone should come and take care of this. I got onto the ticketing system, which asked me if my request was for facilities, security, or one of a list of twenty different choices. You don't commonly encounter raccoons. I actually had no idea where to file my ticket, but I made an educated guess and filed it under security, which I thought was the best choice.

I very quickly got an answer from the right team—which happened not to be security—who said, "We're on it. It's handled." The ticketing system used a prediction engine to make this happen. The system had taken the history of all the tickets ever submitted by employees and fed all that text into the machine learning model. The system looked in particular at which department closed each ticket, assuming that whatever department closed the ticket was the correct department to handle the issue.

If I had sent the raccoon issue to the kitchen staff, the kitchen staff might have reassigned it to facilities, then facilities may have reassigned it to another department, and so on and so forth. It would have eventually gotten to the right place. What Google's model did instead was ask, where did each of the tickets submitted end up? When I filed the ticket, I listed a specific department, which happened to be the wrong one, but by analyzing the data the ticket contained, the system knew what the right department was. Now when users file tickets, they no longer need to assign them to a department in the first place, because machine learning has enough data to analyze where they should be assigned.

At this point, the prediction API has been replaced by a cloud learning model, but the example still illustrates the power of machine learning. Rather than letting a human who is not an expert in a certain task, like picking the right department for filing a ticket on an unusual issue, try to figure out what to do, the machine looks at and sorts through the historical data. This example, by the same token, once again illustrates the fact that the machine had to be trained through the input of thousands of resolved tickets, including data about which department had resolved each issue.

BID MANAGEMENT

Let's return to Smart Bidding and why machines are so much better at bid management than you are. Remember, every Google search triggers an ad auction based on the keywords the user typed in. The bidders are all the advertisers who want their ads to appear when that keyword is used in a search. At the time of the auction, Google considers all the signals or data involved in the search: the user's location, the locations of the advertisers, the time of day, current weather conditions, and so on. At one point, we even considered using the lunar cycle as a factor, but it turned out that the lunar cycle didn't impact likely clickthrough rates, so we tossed it out as a meaningless factor.

Google looks at all the defined factors and then decides on each advertiser's rank. This plays out in relationship to the maximum bid and quality score, since every ad has a quality score that gives the likelihood it will be clicked on, which is also known as the predicted clickthrough rate or pCTR. This is combined with the maximum amount the advertiser is willing to pay if someone clicks the ad. Those two factors give you your rank in the auction and also determine the price you will have to pay when and if you get a click.

There's a difference between the maximum bid, the maximum cost-per-click (CPC) that you're willing to pay, and the CPC you actually do pay. The actual CPC gets discounted as your quality score goes up.

When it comes to bidding, advertisers need to calibrate CPC back into their business goal, which is profitability. This leads to an important distinction in digital marketing. Traditionally, the money in marketing budgets has not necessarily been spent to generate direct returns. It's often about branding. Search marketing, however, is more like direct-response advertising. You're putting in money with an expectation it's going to return a direct result. Search marketing is actually much more like having a sales team rather than a marketing team. The question becomes: how much am I willing to pay my sales team to drive sales for me? Usually you want to make a profit, so you're not going to pay your sales team the full amount of the sale.

If you know your margin or profit on an item needs to be ten dollars, what can you afford to pay for a click? You have to know what your probable conversion rate is: how many clicks you need to get one sale. That probability varies from one keyword to another and from region to region. Bid management therefore becomes very complex, but the bottom line is figuring out what your CPC bids need to be to help you achieve profitability.

In the early days of AdWords, you would have to figure out your maximum CPC and give that figure to Google. You'd probably set a different maximum CPC for every keyword. In the current Google Ads machine learning or Smart Bidding environment, you tell the system what your goal is instead. Of course, your goal is to maximize value, but the system requires you to set some parameters. One parameter might be a 200 percent return on ad spend. In other words, for every dollar you spend, you want a two dollar return in conversion value.

Google then handles automated bid management. In any given auction, based on your parameters, Smart Bidding figures out what you can actually pay in this specific instance to keep you within your specified target. The auction determines which ads are shown on each results page, as well as the placement of your ad on that page.

However, quality score (QS) also factors in here. From Google's perspective, the ads on a page should be at least as useful or relevant as the organic, non-advertising search results. To be placed above organic results, ads need to cross certain thresholds. There's a fairly high bar to be met in terms of ad quality or relevance.

If winning an auction was determined solely on CPC, generally the larger companies with bigger budgets will always win. This isn't good for Google, nor is it good for advertisers, especially smaller ones.

If, this year, there are twice as many searches as the year before, Google's business goal is to make roughly twice as much money this year. The problem is that if advertisers are charged purely on a cost-per-click basis and there's no QS forcing ads to be relevant, there is no guarantee whatsoever that Google's goal will be met, because there's no guarantee that twice as many searches would also lead to twice as many clicks.

Say, for example, a large advertiser, such as an auto manufacturer selling a big pickup truck, says that it is going to bid $100 for any and every keyword in existence. The ad for the truck will appear in first or a high position in every single search. However, it will be irrelevant for almost all of them, so it wouldn't be clicked on, and Google wouldn't make any money.

This is where quality score comes in. In almost every case, the pickup truck ad would be irrelevant, so it will get a low QS. By bringing relevance into the equation, Google is effectively saying that your ad placement is a combination of how much you're willing to spend for each individual click and also how often you get a click when your ad is shown.

The following figure illustrates this process.

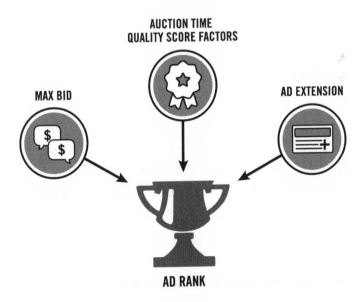

This system is effective for advertisers as well as Google. Unless you're doing branding, which is rarely the case with PPC advertising, advertisers don't want to pay for impressions (CPM); they want to pay for clicks (CPC). As has been mentioned, PPC is basically a sales, not a marketing, engine. It makes sense that you only pay when a user says, "This looks relevant to me. I want to see more." Users are also happy, because QS weeds out ads that look like ads and feel like they're pushing something they don't actually care about. It eliminates the problems that made the banner ads of the late '90s and 2000s so ineffective.

Now, your client doesn't have to be the company with the deepest pockets to get the best position for its ads. The advertiser in first position could actually be paying less than the advertiser in second position, provided the first ad has a higher quality score. If you take the time to create a better ad, you can beat the company willing to spend more for a click but who hasn't spent as much time or effort optimizing its text. While PPC professionals focus on improving quality score by writing more com-pelling text and choosing better keywords, machines are better at the tedious work of determining the right bid for a specific auction.

Because all bid-management computation is handled by machine learning, your time is freed up to think about the creative aspect of both your ads and the landing pages to which they lead. One critical focus is optimizing your landing pages for mobile devices. You might get a click, but if your mobile landing page loads too slowly or otherwise delivers a sub-optimal user experience, people will drop off, and you're going to lose a potential customer. To illustrate this, a 2017 study by Akamai found that conversion rates dropped 7 percent if a landing page loaded 100 milliseconds slower.

Google Ads's quality scores are fundamentally a wisdom-of-the-crowds system. It's been consistently demonstrated that you will get better predictions if you ask a large number of people for their opinions, and then average them out, rather than asking a single specialist what they would predict. Every time a search occurs, people basically vote on ads by clicking on them.

Quality score looks at clickthroughs as a primary indicator of relevance. It also looks at landing pages, which, while clearly important, are secondary rather than primary relevance indicators. If users click on an ad they find compelling, only to end up on a bad landing page, their first thought is, "They've tricked me." They won't trust the advertising any longer. If users click on an ad and then quickly leave the site their click has taken them to, the quality score goes down.

Ultimately, Google's goal is to provide the best user

experience, which means above all else the most relevant search results. A lot of people don't believe that's true, but if you think about it, the only reason Google has become such a big business is because people like and therefore trust their search results. If Google doesn't do a good job with search results, people are going to stop looking to it for answers, which will shrink its business. Google will forgo potential revenue if such revenue has a long-term negative impact on people's trust of their search results. Preventing this is what the quality score system is all about.

BUDGET AUTOMATION

Bid size and budget obviously often go closely hand in hand, as budget is one of the parameters determining how much you are willing to spend to achieve your advertising goals. Smart Bidding figures out how to use that budget to drive clicks and conversions, utilizing the kinds of mathematical optimization models that machines are really good at.

Business goals, however, need to be put in place to constrain the system. As long as you are getting profitable conversions, why wouldn't you buy as many as you can? However, advertisers don't have unlimited budgets, nor, for that matter, do they have unlimited inventory. I remember a high-end custom-gaming computer builder once frantically calling AdWords to say, "Please shut off the ads because we've run out of computers." There are real-world constraints that the system needs to be made aware of.

These constraints all involve dividing budgets up into different categories. For instance, a car dealership might have a certain budget to spend on advertising new cars and a different one for used cars. Different product lines have different profitability rates. Certain times of the month or year might be more profitable than others.

People tend to want to be personally involved in tweaking budgets to hit those milestones. However, it's certainly possible to program such real-world constraints into a Smart Bidding system. Logically, therefore, from the perspective of making as much money as possible, people should be much more hands-off on budgets and let the machine handle them.

Also, on the budget side, one of the premises of the Google machine learning system is that there is a rising complexity in the channels you can advertise on. If you're an e-commerce advertiser, in the past, you've set up separate campaigns to target searches, YouTube, remarketing, and the display network. Now, you have four campaigns with four individual budgets. How you shift funds from one budget to another is something that machines can do faster and more frequently than humans.

This is the premise of Google Smart Shopping campaigns. The advertiser tells Google Ads the budget for the campaign as a whole, and the system will figure out which channels to allocate the budget to in order to get the best value for your business. The system also realizes that these channels interact with one another. If a potential customer begins searching on YouTube, that will probably impact later searches. The customer might end up on your remarketing list if they clicked on an ad that led them to visit your website. Figuring out how to allocate a budget based on all those parameters is complicated.

Machines are also better than humans when it comes to scalability and complexity. There are potentially thousands of scenarios involving a specific potential customer encountering a specific ad or ad variation at a specific time and place on a specific device. People are still better at providing the creative elements that the system can then test. They can also do large-scale targeting. If you are selling disability insurance, you do not want to target people under the age of eighteen who are probably not working yet. However, once such macro-targets have been established, machines are much better than humans at the micro-targeting machine learning has now made possible.

People do not have the time and capacity to manage so many variations and segments. Their capacities are much more in line with the three key roles in which PPC professionals need to position themselves in the new machine learning environment: what I call the "doctor," the "pilot," and the "teacher." Each of these roles will be explored in the following chapters.

POSITION YOURSELF: THREE KEY ROLES

DOCTOR

Machines do some things better than people, and people do other things better than machines. This is an unsurprising, indeed seemingly obvious observation, but one that's often lost sight of in the midst of the "end of the world" attitudes that PPC machine learning seems to promote. In this part, we'll look at the roles marketing professionals, rather than machine learning systems, will continue play in PPC advertising: roles I call the "doctor," "pilot," and "teacher."

You are probably familiar with and are already playing one or more of these roles. You may want to double down your focus on these, however, as they encompass the "human factor" machine learning is unlikely ever to replace. "Doctor," the first of these roles, sub-divides into two related categories: Marcus Welby, MD, the kindly family physician, and Dr. House, the Sherlock Holmes-like forensic pathologist.

MARCUS WELBY, MD, FAMILY PHYSICIAN

If you are an agency owner or independent PPC consultant, the "doctor" role is one you've almost certainly been playing for some time. IBM's Watson or a similar system may now or may soon be able to make a faster, more accurate cancer diagnosis than a family physician or oncologist. Watson, however, has no bedside manner. Only a human doctor has the empathy to deal with the problems and issues that such a diagnosis involves.

Like doctors and their patients, only PPC professionals can truly understand clients and their needs. To be compassionate and understanding, you have to be able to connect the dots and see the whole picture. Clients often ask, "Here are the problems we're facing. What course of action would you recommend?" These problems' causes are not always immediately obvious. However, like a doctor who has seen similar patients and kept up with the latest trends, it's your extensive PPC experience that will enable you to come up with solutions.

As in this example, a doctor's job also involves delivering bad news. Some advertiser clients have goals that are simply not reachable, for whatever reason. You, as the doctor, have to explain both why that's so and what the next best outcome might be if the client is willing to change some parameters and expectations. You also need to be able to identify and explain the tools and methods that can attain that modified goal.

Once after surgery, I ended up with an infection around the sutures. I saw my doctor, who went through a list of five different antibiotics he could give me. While doing so, he was looking at me closely, gauging how bad the infection was, as well as what my physical condition was otherwise. He asked me questions about my lifestyle, including my work and travel schedule. Only then could he say, "Given the various possible side effects and how these might affect your life right now, this is probably the best antibiotic to give you for your infection." He personalized the treatment. If another patient had come in with similar symptoms, he might have chosen a different medication.

When a client comes in with PPC ailments you've seen in other accounts, you draw on your past experience but modify your recommendations based on the specifics of the case. What campaign strategy will work best? What suggestions will this particular client best respond to? This is very much part of the human equation. "Hand-holding" may sound a bit dismissive but is actually a key and very important part of the job.

On another hand, a machine learning system, when consulted for the same problem, would inevitably go for the most aggressive course of action, because, all other things being equal—which they never are—it has the highest chance of quick success. The machine learning system's approach won't account for the personal impact or some of the specifics of the situation.

I might have had an international business trip coming up that my doctor took into consideration when making his prescription. Your client might be launching a new product and can't aggressively change their PPC strategy until after the launch. You have to ask questions and understand your client to make the right decisions and recommendations. In some cases, this requires that you change your "doctor" role from kindly family physician to forensic pathologist.

DR. HOUSE, FORENSIC PATHOLOGIST

In Optmyzr, we have a tool called the PPC Investigator that allows an advertiser to ask general questions about why their business outcomes have changed from one period to the next. A typical question might be, "Why do I have fewer conversions this quarter than I did in the same quarter last year?"

The tool does a root-cause analysis and comes up with one

or more diagnoses. Perhaps you got fewer clicks because fewer people are searching for what you are advertising. You may have lowered the amounts you're willing to bid and have gotten fewer impressions as a result, while your competitors got more of the impressions you would otherwise have received. Your conversion rate might also have gone down because you made a change to your landing pages that makes them less compelling than before.

The client then logically asks, "You just pointed out three significant problems. I've only got a limited amount of time and money at the moment. What's the one thing I should do that would have the greatest effect?"

In one case, the client was a startup that had been able to make changes to its landing page very quickly and on the fly. However, the account manager also knew the company had recently been acquired by a large corporation where policies were much more rigid. Unless that information had been input specifically, it's unlikely a machine learning system would be able to figure out that the business had been recently acquired by a new owner whose priorities were different from the former management team.

If the question had been asked a few months earlier, the answer might have been: let's make some changes to the landing pages. However, the account manager knew that the new owner had a very rigorous process for changing company web pages. In fact, the corporation had a complicated, fifty-page brand-guideline document that covered the specifications for every change down to the pixel, including image content and color-coding.

Given current restrictions, the account manager knew better than to revise the landing pages. The suggestion then became, "Let's change the keyword mix, because that's what we can do right now that will have an impact and start moving things in the right direction." Down the line, other changes might still be made. At the moment, it was critical to prioritize action based on feasibility. This is the kind of flexible approach that account managers, who speak with their clients frequently and take a real interest in what is happening to their businesses, are able to take.

Another important aspect of "bedside manner" or "hand-holding" is the ability to explain the rationale behind a recommendation. Once machine learning is applied to a problem, you can see if it was resolved or not, but the system is generally very bad at explaining exactly *how* the solution was arrived at. If the client asks, "How do I apply this solution to another business where I'm encountering a similar problem?" the system can't respond intelligibly.

The classic example here is asking a machine learning

system to look at a photo and tell you if it is a cat. The system can respond, "Yes, it's a cat." If you then ask, "Well, why is it a cat?" the machine can only respond, "I don't know why. It just is a cat." This is the prototypical black box problem.

However, if you ask a person, "Well, why do you say that's a cat?" you will get a response such as, "It's got pointy ears, little whiskers, and four legs. It looks like a cat." We may not be perfect, but humans are generally much better able to explain how a certain decision was arrived at than a machine is.

Medical patients hate black boxes. "Yes, I'm better. Thank you. But how exactly did these medications make me better? How do I prevent this from happening again?" Doctors need to be able to explain.

When you think about machine learning problems and the engineers working on them, the image that comes to mind isn't warm and fuzzy. It's more: let's figure out the most efficient manner possible of getting that car to drive itself without hitting anyone. However, if you want the public to buy self-driving cars, someone needs to explain how the car's computer is paying attention to what it needs to pay attention to. Here's how the car works, and here's why you might consider buying and using one. It's all about putting a human face on what's happening and taking the driver's (or potential self-driving car owner's) concerns and feelings into account.

It's the same with PPC machine learning systems. Whether a PPC machine learning system is or is not able to solve a problem, the client wants to know how and why. The account manager needs to be able to answer that the machine learning system used such-and-such technique to address the problem, and that's why it did so well. By the way, this other technique that was unable to solve the problem was also investigated and discarded for the following reasons. Now the client has information that can be leveraged. When a similar problem occurs, less experimentation is needed, and the desired outcome is arrived at more quickly. The ability to deliver clear and convincing explanations develops trust.

Researchers have seen that when machine intelligence is applied to a problem, people have very little patience if the desired result is not achieved. If a proposed solution fails, people will quickly say, "Automation doesn't work. Let's give up on it."

That's completely different from how a human would treat a fellow-human coworker. If you get someone to do manually what a machine learning system would have done through automation, they are going to make just as many mistakes—probably more—than the computer would. People tend to forgive those mistakes, however, because they can interact and talk with the coworker. Especially if the coworker has just started a job, this is all an expected part of the learning curve.

Like a quarterback explaining why a game was lost, a smart coworker will say, "I acknowledge that bids were too low because I didn't pay enough attention to the target CPA. I apologize. I'm not going to let this happen again. Please give me another chance." You would probably reply, "You've learned an important lesson and your apology is accepted. Go back and try again."

There's the opposite reaction to a computer. If a computer fails once, you tend not to give it a chance to try again, because it can't really explain itself. As machine learning becomes increasingly important, there's a risk that people will just write it off if a mistake or inaccuracy occurs. That would be a poor decision. Machine learning systems are very powerful and useful but also need to be properly trained. The right training data may not have been input, or a machine learning model may have been deployed in a scenario it was not intended for. However, you don't throw out the baby with the bath water.

Both machines and humans have learning curves. Once, I was brought in to consult with a custom T-shirt company. Their sales volume had dropped off dramatically, and the problem needed investigation. Research showed that what had formerly been their best keywords were no longer producing results. It turned out that the conversion rate had fallen off because they had changed their website design, so they reverted to the old design. Problems persisted, however, because the bid management system had never been told to discount the data from the days when the new landing pages were running. This left the T-shirt company's ads continuing to run on page two, which meant far fewer clicks.

Having done an investigation, I told the client, "Your automated bid-management system was fine, but the data generated during the time you had the new landing pages should have been removed. The system should have been started up again only when things were back to normal."

Ideally, this problem would have been identified and solved at the time it was happening, as you'll see in the next chapter, when we discuss the "pilot" role. However, if a problem persists after its cause was supposedly fixed, you need to play doctor and do more of a forensic investigation. Because of the lapse of time, the cause will probably be less clear than it might have been had it been caught earlier. Deeper research and investigation are then needed, because so much has inevitably changed between the time the mistake was made and when the investigation took place.

You need to become a pathologist like Dr. House, someone with wide knowledge who looks in places other people might not look and considers issues others might not consider. The analogy is more exact than you might think. In PPC, there are so many moving parts that it can be challenging to find what's causing things to go wrong.

I've had a client come to me and ask, "Would you take a look at why this campaign's performance levels have declined?" I looked at the campaign and saw it was full of broad match keywords. As explained above, "broad match keyword" means that Google can show ads not just for a specific keyword, but for closely related keywords. That made it more difficult to answer his question, but PPC professionals who put on their Dr. House hats can come up with the right solution.

By way of example, say the client's broad match keyword was "Xbox games." He decided to reduce his bids from one dollar to fifty cents, and all of a sudden performance dropped. That is to say that, despite reducing the amount he was spending for every click, his cost-per-acquisition had gone up, a counterintuitive result.

However, if you think about it a little more, it makes sense. The reason a keyword is cheap is because advertisers' conversion tracking systems have figured out that a particular keyword yields low performance, so many advertisers may have stopped bidding on it. That's what makes the clicks cheap, because they yield low-quality traffic that is far less likely to convert. So, even though your client is getting more clicks and paying less for each one, he's still going to spend a lot of money, while actually reducing the number of conversions.

What's happening behind the scenes is Google Ads has calculated that since the amount the advertiser is bidding has gone down, his ad is not as competitive as it once was. If the keyword is "Xbox games," they stop showing the ad for queries that are more likely to convert, like "buy Xbox games." The only queries for which they are now willing to show your ad for are ones that are less likely to convert, like "rip-off Xbox games" or "free Xbox games" or "used Xbox games." What's happened behind the scenes is that the advertiser is no longer bidding for the same keyword but for lower-quality traffic.

Another factor working in tandem with this has contributed to the problem. Since it's been some time since the issue began, there may be millions of queries to analyze and run comparisons on. There are a lot of moving parts, which makes solving the problem more difficult—but not impossible.

The solution is a matter of using the experience and intuition gained from many years in the PPC business to progressively narrow down the possibilities, always keeping in mind that what the client is really interested in is not the details but overall trend lines in the KPIs he really cares about.

The doctor role sometimes means playing Dr. House and sometimes playing Marcus Welby. We'll return to Marcus Welby hand-holding "soft skills" in the later chapters on positioning and repositioning your agency. Now, it's time to talk about another role only people can play in PPC marketing: the "pilot."

PILOT

A major part of a PPC account manager's job is to stay on top of things. How is the account performing? Are there any problems or anomalies surfacing that need to be attended to? This is what I call the "pilot" role. A machine can't play this role, because it involves intercepting and solving problems the machine learning system may have caused in the first place.

As with the doctor, there are two aspects to the pilot role. The first is dealing with day-to-day and hour-by-hour oversight. The other involves a more proactive, competitive approach. Let's call the first role the "commercial pilot" and the second the "fighter pilot."

COMMERCIAL PILOT

In today's automated environment, on average, the pilot

of a commercial jet has actual control of the plane, flying it manually, for only eight minutes of every flight. This does not mean the pilot is unimportant, and very few of us would be comfortable getting on a plane that did not have a human pilot to take over when and as necessary.

The most vivid example of this is the famous incident on January 15, 2009, when US Airways Flight 1549 was disabled minutes after taking off from New York's LaGuardia Airport after striking a flock of geese. Pilot "Sully" Sullenberger, trained in the Air Force, was able, through quick thinking and expert maneuvering, to land the plane on the Hudson River, saving the lives of all passengers and crew.

This would not have been a good scenario for a self-driving system to try to land the plane. Human ability and intervention prevented a tragedy. Although the stakes may not be life-and-death, PPC requires human account managers to play a similar role, one that most PPC managers are already familiar with.

There are bound to be deviations from the norm in any PPC campaign, whether automated or manual. Say a news story comes out that relates to one of your client's keywords. Although you didn't know the story was going to appear, you see a spike while monitoring traffic and can then react to the good news by increasing budgets so you can capture all the additional volume. The machine learning system will not learn about the news story until it is too late, if at all.

Conversely, if a news story makes traffic increase but conversions decrease, you may want to reduce budgets and bids until the news cycle plays out and things return to normal. One example with a lot of dark humor was a news story about a man killing his wife, hacking her body to pieces, and putting them all in a certain brand of luggage. There might well be an ad for that brand of luggage next to the story, because the system has been instructed to show ads for that brand on pages that mention suitcases.

Someone might click on the ad out of morbid or bemused curiosity but is unlikely to buy a suitcase. A story about a murder involving your client's brand of suitcase may be "relevant" but is probably not the best place to show your ads. People are not looking at the article because they want to buy a suitcase and are doing research into which brand to purchase. Better to intervene manually and fix the inappropriate targeting before it tarnishes your brand.

Also, as the levels of machine learning and automation increase, problems can arise much more quickly. There are many examples of this, one of the most dramatic being the mini-crash of the NASDAQ stock-trading system on August 22, 2013. The automated trading system was stuck in a self-reinforcing loop, and the market was quickly collapsing. NASDAQ shut down for a little over three hours to figure out what was happening. It undid the erroneous bids that had occurred, hit reset, and opened the market back up.

By way of analogy, on a recent weekend, I had to cut a piece of wood in two. I had two options. If I used my manual saw, it was going to take me five or ten minutes to cut through the wood. I also had an automated saw that spins thousands of times per minute and would take far less time to cut the wood. Which should I use?

I decided to use the manual saw. I didn't feel that I really knew what I was doing with the automated one and figured that, if I used it, there was a small chance I'd injure myself, perhaps badly. So, I took the slow approach because I wasn't planning to cut all that much wood, and learning to use an electric saw safely would have taken more time than cutting the wood I needed manually. Safety first!

When things get faster and faster, as they do with machine learning, there is a more significant potential for sudden crisis. It's important that you have a sense of how these tools work and what might be going wrong, so that you can respond quickly.

Let's return to the example of self-driving cars. One

reason that they aren't yet ready for prime time is their LIDAR image-processing systems. LIDAR is an acronym for "light detection radar." A LIDAR beam is shot onto a surface and bounces back to a machine learning system that analyzes patterns in the visual data and reconstructs an image of the surface.

LIDAR can and has done some amazing things. There's a story about an archeologist who was in a Central American jungle, only thirty feet from a major find, and unable to see it because it was completely hidden by vines and other foliage. A LIDAR beam, however, created a clear image of the Mayan temple hidden underneath. (See: https://www.cbsnews.com/news/mayan-ruin-discovery-lidar-laser-technology/.)

Unlike a self-driving car, a Mayan temple isn't moving. LIDAR works wonderfully in such static situations. It also works fairly well when mounted on a vehicle that is moving but not very fast. If the vehicle starts to go over thirty miles an hour, however, the system doesn't work very well anymore.

This problem is related to speed. Google Smart Bidding works very fast, changing your bids on the fly for every auction. Such a system needs to be monitored or piloted, because things that move fast can also break or go wrong quickly.

To get more specific, say you have a bid-management system that has been working fine. Then let's say you change your client's landing pages or make another change to the website that causes it to go down for a couple of hours. All of a sudden, the bid-management system notices that your conversion rate has been tanking. In a case like that, the system reduces your bids, and those bids become too low to qualify your ad to appear on the first search-results page. The ad now shows up on page two, and nobody—that is, fewer than 5 percent of users—goes to page two anymore. You're in a tailspin.

You or one of the other human pilots on your team notices that the website has gone down, so you bring it back online. As in a previous example, you may think that everything's fixed but have neglected to let the bid-management system know what just happened. The bid management system keeps generating page-two bids because it hasn't received the data that things are fixed, and bids should be increased. These are the issues a PPC "pilot" needs to stay on top of.

The problem is the speed with which these systems work. If you're not on top of things every hour, they might go out of control. However, there's another factor to be considered, which is that you want to be cautious about when you sound an alert.

This is a problem that is particularly acute in hospitals.

Overreaction often leads to false positives: too many alerts about situations that are not genuine emergencies. It becomes hard to distinguish between what really needs attention and what doesn't. If there are too many alerts, the nurses eventually stop hearing them. People occasionally die in hospitals because a true positive—a genuine emergency—wasn't attended to as a result.

As a pilot, how do you learn to pay attention to the problems that really matter? Some of this has to do with the sensitivity of the alert system, just as it would on a commercial jet. Optmyzr has built scripts—miniprograms—that will tell you if there's an anomaly in your account. You can also set KPI alerts once you've determined reasonable sensitivity levels.

Determining when and how to monitor the system manually comes down to some very simple questions. Do you even care if your account is monitored at 1:00 or 2:00 a.m.? Perhaps not, because the traffic volume is going to be minimal. If an anomaly occurs at 2:00 a.m., it may mean there were five instead of ten clicks. If you look at it as a 50 percent drop, it's a big deal. But in absolute terms, it's just five clicks, and that probably isn't something worth setting an alarm or getting out of bed for.

The situation at 10:00 a.m., when people in your market are doing a lot of searches, is quite different. In that case, an anomaly might mean that your ad is down from 1,000 to 500 clicks. Five hundred fewer clicks may hurt your sales for the day and is probably something worth paying attention to.

Part of your job as pilot is to figure out what sensitivities to set. Where do you really need to focus your attention? Let's return to and expand on the ski resort example. A ski resort needs to factor how much snow has fallen in the last twenty-four hours or seven days into its PPC campaigns. You may need to add this factor into the Google Ads Smart Bidding system, which might not otherwise take it into account.

Perhaps a lot of snow has just fallen, which causes you to change your bid strategy. Then you realize the snow that fell was mushy rather than powder. Snow fell, but the temperature was not much below freezing, so its quality wasn't very high. Unless you also take this into account, you will be bidding more than you should have, given the actual scenario. Part of the pilot's role is vetting the system to see that it is taking account of all the important factors in order to course-correct when required. Because the world is an unpredictable place, some of this must be done on the fly.

A commercial pilot follows very regular procedures. These used to be stored in huge binders but are now on iPads or other tablets. For every eventuality, the procedure manual tells you the multitude of things you need to do in which exact order within a specific time frame. Everything a pilot does is scripted at that level. You are there to follow those procedures and make sure all systems are operating properly.

Lufthansa goes even further, taking this out of the cockpit into the cabin. If you, as a passenger, look at the Lufthansa emergency procedure card, it tells you exactly how many seconds you have to put on your oxygen mask once it falls from the ceiling.

Imagine you are the pilot of a PPC campaign. A client comes to you and says, "We have a little bit extra in our budget that we need to spend by the end of the month. What should we do?" What do you do? Do you take the automated bidding system offline and manually boost your bids for the period? Do you go into the campaign settings and adjust budgetary rather than bid parameters?

Your client will tell you what the goal is. However, only you, the pilot, know what those 200 crazy buttons on the ceiling of your cockpit do and which ones to push to achieve the desired outcome. If you don't know off hand, you probably have your agency's procedure binder, which gives you a checklist of five questions to ask the client in such and such a scenario, as well as how to tweak the

Google Smart Bidding system to achieve the desired outcome based on the answers to your questions.

It all goes back to the example of the commercial pilot who only actually flies the plane for eight minutes out of the twelve hours it takes to go from California to Europe. As the PPC manager, most of your job is to monitor the system, making sure it doesn't break. Then, when a request for a change is made, it is your job to deal with the complex task of making sure things are set up so as to achieve the desired outcome.

FIGHTER PILOT

On July 7, 2017, a potential aviation catastrophe at San Francisco Airport was narrowly averted. An Air Canada flight came within thirty feet of landing on top of four planes waiting on one of the airport's runways for takeoff. SFO's Airport Surface Surveillance Capability (ASSC) system, the first installed in the US, lost track of the airplane during several critical seconds. At the time, only one controller, instead of the mandated two, was monitoring tower and ground frequencies. The pilot of the first plane in line to take off sounded an alert, the Air Canada flight pulled up and out, and there were no casualties.

This sort of collaborative scenario is not the norm for PPC campaigns. Advertisers want to beat, not help, their competitors. The PPC manager's role sometimes takes on the characteristics of a fighter pilot, rather than the commercial pilot whose first priority is avoiding accidents. Another analogy is that of the quarterback of a football team. In the midst of a game or a military action, both the quarterback and fighter pilot need to be able to bring all their experience into play in the midst of a constantly changing situation in which their opponents are trying to gain an advantage.

A fighter pilot and a quarterback both take advantage of their opponents' blunders. Similarly, smart PPC managers act when they spot opportunities. You may see a competitor over-relying on automation and can step in to take advantage. Even if you do not want to take offensive action against your competitors, you will need to be able to take defensive action when you find yourself under attack. The fighter pilot's monitoring function is similar to the commercial pilot's but deployed differently.

Let's return to the example where one campaign's bids, because of an error, were lowered to the point where its ads were relegated to the second search-results page. If you were that advertiser's competitor, this would present an opportunity for you to get more clicks at a much lower cost. If you took advantage of the situation quickly enough, you could obtain enough data and maybe even drive enough cheap conversions to get a big enough financial gain to enable you to keep on doing this, at least for a time, even after the other advertiser has corrected the mistake. This requires you to think quickly, to know what to do, and how to act on it.

In many instances, a human PPC manager is better able to exploit a competitive advantage than an automated or machine learning system. I live in Silicon Valley and like to get around on my bicycle. One day I was biking and had to make a left turn across four lanes of traffic. I saw a Google self-driving car coming towards me but decided to cut in front of it. I knew the car's machine learning systems have rules in their programming about not killing bicyclists. I thought to myself, "I know this is cutting it close, but I also know what the car is going to do if I cut in front of it." As an aggressive human cyclist, I was able to beat the car's predictable programming.

A counter-example also involving a self-driving car and a bicycle had a far more tragic outcome. In March 2018, an experimental Uber self-driving car killed a pedestrian in Tempe, Arizona, the first fatal accident of its kind.

Broadly speaking, self-driving systems operate on a three-step process: perceive, plan, and execute. The system perceives what is in front of and around it, makes plans on what to do based on those perceptions, and then executes that plan, putting the wheels in motion, turning the steering wheel if required, and so on.

On the night in question, a woman was walking her bicycle across a four-lane road after dark. The self-driving car's LIDAR perceived the woman, but that's when things went wrong. The perception was "here's a human with a bicycle." However, when the system got to the planning stage, the response was, "This can't be a human with a bicycle. This is a high-speed road. It's the middle of the night. A pedestrian has never been seen in this situation before. The perception must have been wrong." When the execute system asked, "What should we do?" the answer was, "Just keep going." This failure happened because the real world is unpredictable, and the machine learning model, at this point in its development and training, was unable to process this unpredictability. It literally didn't compute.

On a less tragic, more competitive level, the message is clear. Machine learning systems can make mistakes, and it's possible to outflank the competition by capitalizing on them.

Let's go back a few years before machine learning started to dominate PPC. In the old days, there was a strategy called bid-jamming. Everyone was doing manual cost-per-click bidding at that point. GoTo, which was still around and an important player at the time, discounted the top advertiser's bids to the minimum amount required to maintain its position, which was basically one penny more than the bid of the advertiser who was second in line.

What the number two advertiser would then do was keep increasing its bids to just one penny below those of the number-one advertiser, which guaranteed that the number one advertiser was bidding and paying the maximum possible price. The number-two advertiser was basically trying to bleed its competitor dry, so its budget would run out. The number-two advertiser would overtake the number one and then quickly reduce its bids so it couldn't be bid-jammed. Winning PPC auctions is like a competitive game, a situation in which opposing players will try to gain advantage by hook or by crook.

Over time, bid-jamming became less and eventually not at all possible, because the Google AdWords system made the amount of money being spent on bids less transparent. However, there is still a lot of gaming the system going on, and there is no reason to believe that this is going to stop even as it becomes more automated.

There's no reason to think that competitors couldn't take advantage of such current bid strategies as target cost-per-acquisition or target return-on-ad-spend (ROAS), the way bid-jamming was deployed in the past. To return to an earlier example, if an advertiser decides to have a flash sale, the machine learning system may not pick up on the unexpected increase in conversion rates quickly enough to change bids to take advantage of the extra opportunity that existed for a limited period of time. However, a competitor paying attention to your sales calendar could jump on the increased search activity your offline promotions are driving and capitalize on it online.

Say a large department store is having a big one-day sale on bedsheets but forgets to change its targets for that period. A smaller advertiser, which also sells bedsheets and knows what their larger competitor is doing, might set more aggressive bids during the competitor's one-day sale. It can now take advantage of the marketing the larger store is doing. The larger store's ads and other marketing initiatives drive up searches for "bedsheets," but the smaller store's ads now appear at the top of page one and may receive more clicks than the larger store's.

To take an historical but still comparable and relevant example, a number of years ago, Sprint was launching a new phone, for which it was meant to be the top but not exclusive vendor. These were the early days of search marketing and they did a multimillion-dollar TV, radio, and print—but NOT online!—campaign around the launch. AT&T and Verizon realized that Sprint was going to pay for a big campaign and decided to take advantage. They bought PPC ads on the appropriate keywords, on which they bid aggressively to scoop up numerous conversions at the bottom of the funnel. They were thinking, "Thank you, Sprint, for spending millions of dollars to get people to come and do searches for the keywords you're letting us buy cheaply. Thanks for doing all that work for us!"

One Google Ads automated bid-management innovation is called Target Outranking Share. What that means is that you, as an advertiser, can stipulate that you want to have your ad show in a higher position when your competitor is a certain advertiser you specify. In that case, Google will automatically raise your bids so that your ad stays ahead of the ads from the specified competitor.

However, what if that competitor does the same to you? Now the bids just keep shooting up. Who wins? Google wins; relatively speaking, both you and your competitor lose. Eventually, one of you is going to get the desired result, but only at a high cost.

A smarter and more defensive approach would be to set limits on how much you are willing to spend to outrank your competitor. As long as you haven't set any stupid bid values, when you win, you actually win. Google is very happy, you are relatively happy, and your competitor, which has lost, is unhappy.

One essential defensive maneuver is avoiding what I call vanity bidding in general and target outranking bidding in particular. Target outranking is generally about visibility, not about connecting the dots to your profitability or sales goals. It's literally saying, "I want my ad to come up before my competitor's." But what does that do for you? Are you trying to buy brand? If so, are you really going to be able to compete on brand against someone who may have already spent much more on their brand efforts?

Fighter pilots cannot be stupid actors. There are the logical moves we know we should make, but vanity and vanity bidding just aren't logical. On the one hand, as shown earlier, even if it sounds too high and makes you uncomfortable to pay Google fifty dollars for a click, it may make sense to pay that much, if I can show you that the math says you are going to make a profit on these expensive clicks because they'll lead to enough high-value conversions.

Conversely, there are other advertisers who reverse that and say that it doesn't matter if they pay fifty dollars per click—even if it makes no economic sense—because "I just want to be in first position." If you run the math with them, you might say, "Well, honestly, based on your conversion rates, you can only afford to spend two dollars for a click." But illogical vanity kicks in. Your client wants to be in first position just because they need to be at the top, like the plumbers whose company names start with 'AAA...' just so they are the first listed in the Yellow Pages. That made sense when people used the Yellow Pages, but in search marketing, the advertising game is played differently. Obviously, this is your client's decision, but as a fighter-pilot PPC professional, you need at least to advise them what the consequences will be. Google Ads machine learning certainly isn't going to do this. Perhaps your client will see the light, especially if you present the logically convincing argument that there is to be made. Some clients may refuse to follow logic, but you have done your best to save them from themselves.

Conversely, if you find out your competitor is doing vanity bidding, it's quite possible for you, as a fighter pilot, to take advantage of this. For instance, if your competitor's business is smaller than your client's, you can get them to bleed out their entire daily budget by setting aggressive bids yourself.

Once the competitor's budget for the day runs out, your client can easily dominate page traffic for the rest of the day. Even if you reduce the amount of your bids significantly, you are still going to get a ton of traffic. You are willing to lose half the day to bleed your competitor dry and dominate the rest of the day. At that point, you don't have to pay a lot for more traffic, since you've effectively reduced the number of clicks your competitor is getting for its set budget, and yours is now the number-one ad, which will have a higher clickthrough rate than the lower-ranked ads.

Other examples of fighter-pilot strategies come more from the creative side. A competitor could be using your trademark as a keyword, leveraging your brand to get more traffic. There's no law against that—at least in the US—but competitors who use your brand in their ad text in a potentially misleading way is something to watch out for. When you become aware of such a move, you simply inform Google, and they may take down the ad that is using your brand name in its text.

You could also come up with a really strong ad text for a client that everyone starts to mimic. There are third-party competitive-analysis tools out there that will tell you when someone—you or a competitor—changes the call to action in its ad text with excellent results. Any number of advertisers using the same competitive-intelligence tools might say, "That's interesting. Let's try the same call to action."

Of course, when everyone starts to use a similar or identical call to action, it dilutes the uniqueness and value of the original ad, which made it stand out. Now, the imitative ads are just part of the crowd. How quickly do you pick up on and react to that? How do you stay one step ahead of everybody who's playing follow the leader?

First of all, you probably won't pick up on this sort of thing on your own, so you probably need some sort of monitoring and alerting tool to tell you when others start to mimic your ads. You can do that by looking at search results, but you can also put a metrics or KPI indicator in place that tells you that your clickthrough rate is starting to decline. Since, according to the Google Ads terms of service, you're not allowed to scrape Google, scraping Google Ads every hour to look at what your competitors are doing is something you shouldn't be doing if you want to stay in the PPC business. However, you can still look at other signals for anomalies that could be indicators of what your competition is up to.

If everybody begins to mimic your ad, but this is not actually detrimental to your metrics, then there is really not a problem. However, if your clickthrough rates start to falter, even though your ads are still in the same position, that may be an indicator that your competitors are starting to mimic your ads. Set yourself an alert, so you can go and look at what they're doing. You can do a manual search, and if you find that that's exactly what they've done, just stay one step ahead of the curve.

Quickly put your next ad-text experiment into rotation. Clearly, you're good at writing ad text, since you've been able to get the pack to follow you. Now, while everybody else is getting stale, you'll again already be ahead of the pack.

In the commercial pilot role, you need to keep an eye out for problems the machine learning system may be causing and correct them. As a fighter pilot, you try to exploit the mistakes your competitors make.

In the final analysis, machine learning problems can only be fixed with training, and all machine learning systems need to be trained. Only humans can train these systems, and another role PPC professionals can and must take on is "teacher."

TEACHER

One thing I hope this book has made clear about PPC machine intelligence systems—or indeed any AI system— is that like any piece of software, they still need to be created by humans. These systems don't come into existence by themselves, nor do machine learning models learn by themselves. Humans in the "teacher" role must do the system's initial training and continue to refine that training as needed.

As has been discussed, many, if not most, people think of machine learning as a black box, or, putting a more positive but equally confusing and inaccurate spin on this perception, as a system that works by magic. However, as seen in chapter 2, PPC machine learning systems are built and trained with hardcore math, statistics, and computational modeling. When such a system is created, humans still have to write the underlying algorithms. Existing algorithms also need to be enhanced to get the system to look at new factors and be more precise in its predictions. Also, it's humans who can and do come up with entirely new machine learning models.

This seems to be outside the realm of marketing, strictly speaking, but not so far as might be imagined. PPC marketing is much more quantitative than traditional marketing and has become increasingly so over the years. As search engine marketing has developed in the last fifteen years, it has involved an increasing amount of data analysis and works with evermore automated systems. PPC marketing has become somewhat less focused on the creative side and somewhat more on numerical optimization as a result: setting the right bids, putting the right budgets in places, and so on.

BUILDING AND TRAINING

The "teacher" role is particularly relevant for PPC professionals with technology training. If you are a "quant," there is a significant opportunity for you to build the future of PPC machine intelligence, as opposed to being restricted by what others have built or are building.

However, it's important that all PPC managers—whether they're quants or not—understand this role. You don't have to have the training to build a machine learning system from scratch, or even to modify one, but you do have to understand how an existing system is trained with an historical data set. All this ultimately relies on your understanding of who your clients are and what their needs are. What dials might be tweaked to move the needle for them?

For instance, being able to modify bid adjustments is critical in all PPC marketing. Bids are adjusted according to criteria you and your clients set: whether a certain click should be valued more or less highly, given a factor or combination of several factors. Some of the default factors Google Ads allows you to adjust for are where the user is located, the time of day, day of the week, type of device, and such demographics as the user's gender and age range.

When optimizing using large amounts of data, people tend to try to move everything to the average. A good machine learning system shouldn't do this, and it's up to the teacher to make sure it doesn't. In general, what's cheap needs to be bid up, and what's expensive needs to be bid down, but the definitions of "cheap" and "expensive" depend on the factors involved.

Consider the factor of user location. A good teacher realizes there are reasons why certain locations are more expensive than others. For instance, New York will probably be more expensive than Kalamazoo. Sometimes automation systems are built that say, "Find places that are expensive compared to the average and move them down, and things that are cheap compared to the average and move them up, so that everything moves towards the average." You could easily build a rule-based automation that does this. An obvious adjustment would be to reduce New York bids and increase Kalamazoo bids.

This approach ignores the fact that in each location, costs vary in certain verticals and industries. If you are looking to hire a lawyer, you're probably just going to pay more in New York than in Kalamazoo, given, if nothing else, the higher cost of living. Another vertical might be more expensive in Kalamazoo than New York.

As a teacher, you have to decide whether or not to use the "Big Mac" index of purchasing-power parity between different locations in developing or modifying your machine learning model. Is that a good enough equivalent to what PPC bids should cost in your client's specific vertical? Or does your agency have enough clients in the same industry across several different cities that you should build a different baseline? One that would enable the system to understand what the best baseline for the same keyword for the same type of business across different cities and

168 · DIGITAL MARKETING IN AN AI WORLD

different accounts would be, and leverage that to move things in the right direction? The role of the teacher is to define the formula or methodology to be deployed to sensibly address a goal like setting the right bids in the right cities.

There's simple math and there's advanced math. As the human teacher, you have to know which most closely models the real world, while taking such constraints as how much data you have access to into account.

In our example, the machine learning model's baseline is that it "knows" that New York is more expensive than Kalamazoo for certain verticals and vice versa. Instead of having the system adjust bids towards an average, which is the wrong approach in this and many other cases, you can instead ask, "Are we paying the right amount for a click to get a legal lead in New York?" The cost-per-click might be higher than what you would pay in Kalamazoo, but the real issue is whether the cost-per-click is similar to that for other New York lawyers.

A pattern-recognition problem like this is often only solvable with a large amount of data, which in turn can only be processed by a machine learning system. Your agency may already have access to a large amount of data. If not, tool vendors like Optmyzr can be enlisted to provide the necessary additional data and processing power.

BUILDING A MACHINE LEARNING MODEL FOR A PPC PROBLEM

What does it take to go down the path of building a machine learning model to solve a PPC problem? Here's what we went through to establish an algorithm applicable to changing bids for different geographical locations.

We set out to build a tool that recommends bid adjustments in different geographic locations to improve performance. But we found that doing a traditional CPA or ROAS target ignores an important element: how expensive a certain region is for a certain vertical. For example, it would be wrong to bid down in San Francisco, because San Francisco is a more expensive market in general. We'd only want to bid down if the actual performance in San Francisco was more expensive than expected.

Humans are good at comprehending and analyzing single- and perhaps two-dimensional data. When there are n features or dimensions to think about and make sense of, things become overwhelmingly complicated. This is where machine learning came to the rescue!

We built a model that generates a campaign's average position based on a number of features and data, including expense of location, expense of a specific vertical, quality score, CPC, and so on. These were analyzed across tens of thousands of accounts and the model used to simulate new average positions that would be attained as a result of making bid adjustments.

This was still not the complete solution. We only had simulations at campaign levels and needed to achieve a similar goal at the account level. We had to figure out which campaigns had to start spending more at specific locations and which campaigns had to start spending less, so that the account's overall number of clicks or conversions could be maximized at the least increase in cost. In computer science, this is called a non-linear fractional knapsack problem, and such problems are hard to solve with traditional algorithms, at least in a reasonable time frame.

We resorted to a Genetic Optimization Algorithm. In computer science and operations research, genetic algorithms (GA) are inspired by the process of natural selection and belong to the larger class of evolutionary algorithms (EA). Genetic algorithms are commonly used to generate high-quality solutions to optimization and search problems by relying on operators inspired by biological processes such as mutation, crossover, and selection. These yield optimal bid-adjustment allocations for a campaign across a variety of geographical locations. This level of intelligence has helped accounts to drive down costs-per-click (CPC) and increase returns-on-ad-spend (ROAS). Coming up with bid adjustments across hundreds of campaign and location combinations is very difficult to achieve manually.

DHIWAKER N. AMARNATH

SOFTWARE ENGINEER, OPTMYZR

BQML

One approach to building your own machine learning models is to leverage Google's BQML feature in conjunction with Google Ads. BQML stands for big query machine learning, and this feature facilitates feeding specific data about your client's business into the system. This includes data about scenarios that have led to the desired outcomes: getting a click and making a sale. After this point, the machine really can start to learn, but only once it has been trained and taught, which means you're inputting the data and real-world examples on which it can build an appropriate model.

Even if you're not a quant who can build machine learning models from scratch, someone at your agency has to be able to modify and adjust the factors those models take into account. Every client will have different inputs, and you will need to account for these different factors in focusing on the desired outcome. Understanding how to properly feed those factors into PPC machine learning models is critical. This is really about asking the right questions and having both the experience and tools, such as BQML, to help you get relevant answers.

Jordan Ellenberg tells an instructive story in his book *How Not to Be Wrong*. During World War II, the military wanted to minimize the chances of airplanes getting shot down. The question became where airplanes should be reinforced to make this less likely. All the airplanes that had bullet holes from being shot at were sitting in hangars. People, who at the time would be the closest thing to data scientists, did an analysis of how many holes there were in each of the airplanes' major parts—wing, engine, fuselage, and so on.

The most bullet holes per square foot were found in the fuselage. The recommendation was that every fuselage be reinforced with extra steel. The entire airplane couldn't be reinforced because then it would be too heavy to fly.

However, a particularly brilliant mathematician named Abraham Wald disagreed. If planes whose fuselages were riddled with bullet holes were able to return to base, the problem couldn't be the fuselage. What the previous researchers had ignored was that it was more important to consider where the planes that never made it back were hit. That was in the engine.

Similarly, PPC professionals need to be able to connect the factors that they know are going to impact their clients' business to the automated systems trained to make predictions. While Google Ads automatically makes adjustments with respect to over 200 factors—including location, time of day, time of week, and demographics—there are undoubtedly other factors and variations that significantly impact your client's business.

The classic, if somewhat overused, example is weather. If your client is a restaurant with a lot of outdoor seating, you will probably have fewer sales on days when it is raining, because no one will want to sit outside. However, if it's a beautiful summer night, everybody will want to sit outside, and you may make twice as many sales without even trying.

How would you tie the weather factor back into how your

advertising dollars are being spent? On a day when it rains, discounts are particularly important. An ad needs to be run saying, "Come by. We've got an amazing happy hour no matter what the weather." On a beautiful night when the restaurant will be packed, because it has a loyal, established customer base, an ad may not need to be run at all and your client can save some money.

Basing your bids on weather intuitively makes sense. But weather involves many sub-factors that will provide different results depending on your business. The restaurant example is fairly simple. If your client is a car dealership, things get more complex. How much does the fact that it's either raining or eighty-five rather than eighty degrees outside impact how many people come to the dealership? It's uncomfortable to stand outside when it's either wet or hot. The problem is that many PPC professionals don't know which questions can be answered and, if they can, how best to arrive at those answers.

BQML affords you a way to plug in known and obvious values, such as how many clicks and how many conversions occurred, to yield predictions. Just as importantly, it enables you to add other interesting data, such as the temperature on the days those clicks and sales occurred. Now the system can do an analysis determining the relevance of those factors. The weather may not be relevant if it's only drizzling, but an inch of rain could have a big impact. So could a five-degree shift in the temperature. You now have insights that can be leveraged to optimize the account.

The point is, even though something may make sense intuitively, you may not know how to get an answer to your question, because you don't know the exact impact a certain factor or sub-factors have. Yes, weather has an impact, but what kind of weather has an impact and how much should that affect your bids and budgets? These are unknowns, and this is where BQML comes in as an off-the-shelf tool that lets you start to dabble with asking these sorts of questions and getting answers you can actually start doing something with.

REGRESSION MODELS

Everything starts with training and then, just as importantly, testing the system so you know it is taking account of the factors you know or discover are important. Doing this properly doesn't require a deeply technical background. Machine learning systems often utilize regression models, and although the term "regression model" may be a bit off-putting, what is required to train them is fairly obvious, since regression models simply show how variables—the various factors important to your client's business—relate to one another.

Websites like Redfin or Zillow use regression models to predict the likely value of your house. What they ask for is the basics. What's the square footage? How many bedrooms? How many bathrooms? How big are the yards? What is the zip code? The system has looked at millions of these data points so as to be able to analyze where your house fits and tell you its value based on those factors.

It is the same with PPC bid management. For instance, you know that people in zip code 94022 tend to buy more houses with four bedrooms than with three bedrooms; they like and are able to afford more space. So, you will want to bid a bit higher for a click from zip code 94022 for a house with four bedrooms than for a house with three bedrooms, and this will become one component factored in when training the system.

SUPERVISED MODELS

When training a supervised machine learning model, you, the teacher, need to give the system the historical—the "supervised" or known—data you believe matters. Such input includes how much your client sold in the past, where the customers who bought the product or service were located, and so on. Every piece of data you feed into the model is structured because it is labeled. One known number represents clicks, another represents conversions, and so on. The machine then predicts how much you can expect to sell, given the similarities and differences between the new and historical data.

Machine learning can deliver new insights because it finds patterns or clusters of similarities. Rather than drawing a hard line, assuming that all users who live in one zip code are going to be better customers than those living in another zip code, the system finds pockets of similarity that may not have been obvious to you, because there is so much more data to consider. In teacher mode, you train the system to find new customers that are somehow similar to your current customers in what may be non-obvious ways. Google's "similar audience" targeting feature is a good example of this.

You are still responsible for inputting as much data as possible on your current customer base, because you want the machine to spot potential new customers based on currently unknown commonalities.

REINFORCEMENT LEARNING

Another increasingly important type of training is called reinforcement learning. As a teacher, your job is no longer to give the system the historical data on past events that will help it predict the future. Rather, it is to tell the system the rules of the game.

The classic example of reinforcement learning is the Bricks Breaking computer game. You have a paddle and little ball that can gradually break through a brick wall. What you tell the computer is that more points will be accumulated if the ball breaks more bricks and doesn't drop to the ground. Those are the rules of the game.

In the beginning, the computer will move the paddle in a very random fashion. As it continues to play, it will realize that if the paddle moves away from the ball, the ball will fall to the ground, no bricks will be broken, and no points awarded.

Now the computer will try something different. It keeps testing different strategies until it figures out that if it always hits the ball, the ball won't fall to the ground and can therefore break more bricks. It also learns that it needs to hit the ball to different parts of the wall to break more bricks. After this point, the whole wall will be quickly broken down and the greatest number of possible points accumulated.

The computer has learned to do this through reinforcement. The point is that the computer learns where to put the paddle, so it hits and doesn't let the ball drop, to break all the bricks and accumulate the most points.

Basically, in reinforcement learning, you define the rules

of the game and then let the computer run simulations to figure out how to win. The same principle is applied to self-driving cars. Given such constraints as the number of self-driving cars and number of hours in the day, there is a limit to how quickly data about how such a car should behave can be made available. That's the reason Google has built simulators.

Now, the self-driving car's machine learning system is basically playing a game. The rules of the game are: stay on the road; don't hit anything; and don't kill anyone. When Google puts its self-driving cars on actual roads, most of the situations they encounter are "normal" and therefore boring. It's only maybe three or four times a day that the car encounters a challenging situation, and the human safety driver has to take over. A simulator can run scenarios, such as what should be done at difficult intersections, thousands of times, so the system quickly learns what it needs to do.

The potential benefit to PPC of reinforcement learning, which involves gamification and running simulators, is that systems can be trained without as much reliance on actual historical data. Such data comes with a hefty price tag. Say your client is a lawyer paying twenty or thirty dollars each time her ad is clicked. If it takes the data from a thousand clicks to enable the computer to make the proper predictions, your client has just spent $20,000.

With reinforcement learning, if you can teach the computer the rules of the game, you can run simulations at a much lower cost. At that point, you let the system loose, knowing it's going to produce good results either immediately or very quickly.

TRAINING QUALITY SCORE

As discussed above, AdWords's first form of machine learning was the Quality Score system, which ranked ads based on the likelihood they'd be clicked on. To train the system, someone on the AdWords team was given a long list of user searches and their results, including the ads that appeared in those results. The team member was then asked to rank an ad on a number of factors. How relevant is this ad to the keywords? How relevant are the text and the landing page? Each factor was given a relevance score of one to five.

One of the keywords evaluated in those days was "iPad," and the ads using that keyword were getting consistently poor scores. This was surprising and counterintuitive. The iPad was a very popular device when it first came out, the first really good tablet computer. However, a lot of phony schemes were devised following its introduction, such as, "Fill out this form and get five of your friends to fill it out, and we'll send you a free iPad." Nobody ever got the free iPad, either because it was ridiculously hard to meet all the requirements, or the offer was simply a scam. These ads were eroding user trust in Google's results, and that had to be addressed.

The team looked at these results and found a pattern. The challenge then became how to automatically identify similar problematic ads, a perfect question for a machine learning system. Based on what they had found, the human teachers gave the system additional data to consider, and, after some time rebuilding its models, the Quality Score system could now attempt to identify this pattern across the billions of ads on Google.

The team would look at these results and ask if the bad ads linked to these keywords had all been found. Have all the bad actors been identified? Generally, there was an improvement, but it was not significant enough. There would still be too many false positives or false negatives. The machine learning model would be updated again, perhaps to weigh factors slightly differently, using an alternative underlying statistical method. After the system had been re-tweaked, there would be another batch of results to review.

Over time, the system continued to improve. Absolute accuracy was not the goal, because it was unattainable. We didn't want the system to penalize advertisers unjustly, and if that meant a few bad actors still got through, that was a price that needed to be paid. The issue was to set a "good enough" performance standard to which the system had to conform.

At that point, the machine could be let go and start teaching itself by analyzing results and learning from its mistakes. The point, however, is that the system didn't build itself. There was a lot of human involvement at the beginning. We asked, "What problems should we look at? How are we going to solve those problems? Once trained, is the system addressing those problems correctly?"

The Quality Score system was trying to predict click-through rates from a data set encompassing a number of different factors. What factors or combination of factors lead to a higher or lower chance of a click?

One example would be the relationship of the location of the person doing the search and the location of an advertiser. A German user could do a search and see ads from vendors in both France and Germany. Presumably, the German advertiser is going to get a higher clickthrough rate from this particular user, because shipping costs from France might be higher, or the user, like many people, prefers to shop locally.

The trick for the human teacher is and will continue to be to figure out which combinations of factors should be considered. Until computing power is so massive that issues of combinatorial explosion are no longer relevant, the system can only consider so many factors, especially if it needs to make predictions near instantaneously. Hence, it needs some human guidance to look at factors most likely to have a meaningful impact.

As mentioned previously, at one point, we decided to see if the lunar cycle was a factor that had any impact on clickthrough rates. It turned out not to, but it was still an appropriate question to ask. And who knows? Perhaps psychics do better business when the moon is full, in which case, if you're building an automated system for your client, it should raise their bids at that time of the month.

Again, you can rely on Google's standard models and hope they take into account the factors that matter to your client. You can use BQML, big query machine learning, to feed the system all the relevant data you feel it should be trained on, because BQML helps you answer the questions: Does my additional data matter? If it does matter, to what degree? And how do I automate these insights?

The analysis system may be able to say, based on today's date, current weather conditions, and maybe even the lunar cycle, that it looks like you're going to have a really good night for conversions. Now you can build an automation or do some manual management that says: based on this, I'm going to set a more aggressive cost-per-acquisition target, because I know we'll have a period of strong conversion rates. On its own, the Google Ads machine learning system won't know this, and by relying on it exclusively, you will come in as a merely average-performance advertiser, far below your actual capacity for delivering the best results.

This is the point that has been frequently made—humans know or have learned something about their businesses that Google Ads system isn't looking for. The human teacher can then bring this into the equation and figure out how to act on it. The results the best PPC managers achieve are not just the Google Ads averages but better. This is what makes you stand out as a "teacher" and extraordinary PPC professional.

DIY

If you're able, you can also be more proactive. If you have the resources and the goal is important enough, there's another more difficult and advanced approach, the one we took at Optmyzr, which is to build your own machine learning models from scratch. This can be thought of as the final stage, in which a teacher with tech training decides what needs to be built from scratch and what can be built by leveraging an existing tool. Again, if you are a "quant," there is a significant opportunity for you to build the future of PPC machine learning, as the field is still in its early stages.

As previously mentioned, a model can best be thought of as a mathematical way to represent the real world. The question then becomes: what machine learning model will best allow automation to understand what drives your client's goals and needs? There is no single right answer, since a model's purpose is to formulate an abstract representation of your business goals that can then generate predictions enabling your client to take the actions necessary to achieve those goals. Depending on what moves the needle for your business, different types of models may prove more or less efficient. Also, keep in mind that no model is perfect, because the real world is highly unpredictable. The best that can be done is to give it some order or structure.

That's basically what self-driving cars are also trying to do. They're never going to be able to account for every single thing that might happen. A favorite example from a while back is when a self-driving car encountered a woman with a broomstick chasing a duck on the sidewalk. The self-driving car completely froze. It had no clue what it was seeing or what was going to happen next, and shut down just to be safe.

Essentially, you, as a PPC professional, are trying to find

or come up with a good representation of your client's business, one that facilitates decision-making. The most likely decisions you need to make are probably, "How much should we bid? How much should we budget? What kind of keywords should we run? How should we change our messaging for different customer segments?" These are the questions that PPC machine learning models will help you answer, but only after they have been properly trained.

The teacher is the third of three roles—the other two being doctor and pilot—that human PPC professionals, not machines, will continue to play in the emerging AI landscape. If you now play and continue to play one of these roles, you are and will remain in a position of strength in the industry.

That's an overview of individual roles in the emerging landscape. Let's now move on to see how PPC businesses—agencies and consultancies—should position themselves in the new world of machine learning.

POSITION YOUR AGENCY: YOUR NEW VALUE PROPOSITION

DEFINING YOUR AGENCY AND ITS VALUE

Part II of this book focused on opportunities for individual PPC marketing professionals to position themselves in the new world of machine learning. Part III will cover how to position your business, whether you are a solo PPC consultant or the owner or a team member of a PPC agency of whatever size—small, medium, or large. How businesses need to position themselves is somewhat different than how individuals should do so.

An agency can be successful in deploying automation at several different levels. Opportunities exist across the board.

As a case in point from a different industry, what do you

think is California's biggest agricultural export? The first answer that came to my mind was wine. Actually, it's almonds. Why? They're very easy to machine harvest. All that needs to be done is shake the tree really hard and gather together the almonds that have fallen to the ground. The process is almost completely automated at this point.

However, not every farmer in California grows almonds. In fact, there has been a dramatic shift in eating habits in the past fifteen years. People want organic foods, and in California and elsewhere, open-air farmer's markets have become popular, both because of the superior produce they offer and the sense of community they foster.

As a farmer, you don't have to be part of a large-scale agri-business in California's Central Valley. If you're a small-scale farmer with a craft business that produces particularly tasty organic tomatoes, you're still looking at a significant, if different and somewhat smaller, opportunity. Your highly desirable and carefully grown crop is bound to command a higher price than automatically harvested crops, such as almonds, that are available in great abundance.

It's the same in PPC marketing. Living in Silicon Valley, I see many people chasing the next unicorn, believing they want to found billion-dollar businesses. In fact, many might be far happier running a smaller company, doing something they're passionate about, rather than running interference against the tremendous competition that arises when you follow everybody else's dream.

This is also true in the PPC business, whether you're a solo consultant or part of an agency. We're now shifting the focus from how you, as an individual, can produce great work within your company to what an agency's business plan and value proposition can be. Obviously, there are differences among agencies with one, twenty, one-hundred, or 1,000 people. However, all agencies and consultants need to retain current clients and find new ones. The question is how you are going to position your agency against all the other available options. What is the unique value proposition you can offer clients and actually deliver on?

No matter what level of automation you deploy or what type of business you want to run—huge or small, a global franchise or boutique agency—there are opportunities across the board. PPC is yet another industry affected by the move to machine learning and AI, but this shift is not necessarily going to be as disruptive as you may fear. However, in all cases, you still need to take the effects of machine learning on PPC into account.

YOUR OLD VALUE PROPOSITION IS TOAST

To put it bluntly, your old value proposition is toast. The PPC landscape is changing so rapidly that what you were selling two years ago is not what is going to bring in sales today. As previously mentioned, Google Ads is doing a great job both building and selling their new Smart machine learning PPC systems—so good that current and prospective clients may now believe agencies and the "human element" no longer play a role important enough to be paid for. To counter such shortsighted attitudes, you need to ask yourself a question that, as a marketing and advertising professional, you really should be able to answer. What's your pitch?

Like it or not, the market is full of buzzwords. Just a couple of years ago, "big data" was what would supposedly make your business hugely successful. Now, everything is about "machine learning" and "artificial intelligence." These trends are related—machine learning makes the processing of big data possible—and are undoubtedly bringing about fundamental changes in PPC.

At the same time, your prospective clients have probably heard the same buzzwords you have whenever they check out the latest software tools and prospective vendors. All your competitors are using these buzzwords as well. Regardless of how and to what degree you see yourself using these technologies, you simply have to be familiar with and take a position on them.

On the other hand, there is a great deal of wisdom in what Jensen Harris, co-founder and CTO of Textio, a company that automates outbound communications and job ads, said in a panel discussion in September 2017: "Saying that you have ML [machine learning] in your product is like saying 'we also have internet.' All software is going to have machine learning, all software is going to have aspects of machine intelligence." If all software is going to have some form of machine learning built in, by extension, the software you are going to be using as a PPC professional is also going to have machine learning, even if it's the latest version of software, such as Excel spreadsheets, that you have already been using for twenty years.

Keep in mind, trying to distinguish your business by touting it as "the machine learning agency" doesn't really mean anything. Every PPC agency is now a machine learning agency. On the other hand, you have to make sure you have a strong position on how machine learning and artificial intelligence fit into your unique value proposition and business offerings. What actually differentiates you from and makes you better than your competitors? Machine learning has become ubiquitous. At some level, everyone has access to it. The differentiator is how you are deploying it to solve problems.

You are not differentiating yourself by saying you're the machine learning agency if all that means is you are using

Google's Smart Bidding. Smart Bidding is a powerful machine learning tool, but one that Google Ads allows every advertiser in its system to use for free. If that's how you're trying to differentiate yourself, the message you are really sending is your agency is no better than average.

You want to be able to tell clients, "We leverage Google's real-time machine learning systems in ways that bring your unique business data more fully into the equation to maximize your PPC results." Now you're not cookie-cutter, doing just what everybody else is doing. You've gone beyond that.

This will often involve identifying and using other third-party tools to leverage the full power of automation. There are many different ways to go about building a superior PPC machine learning system. Smart Bidding looks at a number of factors Google considers important, but you may know there are certain other factors that matter to your clients' businesses. If you have the capability to use software like Tableau to do regression analyses, or R, an open-source statistical software, to figure how much impact specific factors have and the correlation of this impact with other factors, you can feed additional, significant data into Google Smart Bidding. That's going to improve your results dramatically.

It is also critical to back up your assertion of superior

machine learning capabilities with very concrete examples of what you've done. If your prospective client is a hotel company, and you have done research correlating the number and type of events on a ticketing website in a given period in a given location with the likelihood of hotel rooms being booked at certain price points, the client will sit up and take notice. How was the research done? Does your agency employ people skilled in Google's Big Query machine learning system, Tableau, R, Microsoft's Azure, or one of the Amazon machine learning systems?

It's not so much which tool you select as your expertise in using that tool and integrating its results with Google Ads that matters. Your ability to understand the capabilities of these tools and how they interplay with other systems and automations, and how to put things together for the maximum optimization payoff, makes your agency valuable. *That's your value proposition.*

How do you establish the validity of that value proposition? You don't have to be able to build a machine learning system from scratch. It's great if you have this capability, but this is not the only way to differentiate yourself. As previous chapters have shown, knowing how to determine which are the most important factors that need to be taken into account in any given campaign, and the related data that should be used to train the system, are critical in achieving a competitive advantage in the new machine learning environment.

An alternative to "build-from-scratch" involves the powerful "recombinant innovation" strategy, to use a term introduced by Professor Andrew Hargadon of the UC Davis Graduate School of Business Management in his 2003 book *How Breakthroughs Happen: The Surprising Truth about How Companies Innovate.* The default definition of "innovate" is coming up with something completely new. However, innovation is often recombinant, which means taking existing tools and concepts and piecing them together in unique and interesting ways.

This gets very down-to-earth and pragmatic. Say your client manufactures sunscreen. It's quite probable more people buy sunscreen on days when the ultra-violet (UV) index is high. Also remember there are scripts that add weather data to bid management in Google Ads. Let's combine these two notions. Now you should start looking for days when the UV index is high and integrate that factor into the Google Ads bidding system. You may also want to double down on bids in places—such as Australia and New Zealand—where the UV index tends to be consistently high.

As this example shows, it's not necessary for an agency to come up with crazy new approaches to innovate. What is necessary is to know the systems, data, and tools that are out there and what others have done with them, and then to come up with interesting, innovative new combinations and applications.

VALUE PRICING

It's also critical, as an agency, to figure out what your added value is and apply it to the pricing of your offering. The continuing evolution of the technology, some of which is free and some of which involves third-party vendors, impacts how much you should charge your clients. A lot of agencies now charge their clients technology fees. Agencies typically charge 10 percent of ad spend to manage a client's account. Many also charge an additional 5 percent to cover the software or SaaS (software-as-a-service) licenses for tools that make the agency more efficient and more effective, like the software my company Optmyzr makes.

As these technologies become more prevalent and increasingly commoditized, licensing prices will probably go down. There are two responses an agency can take to this, involving business decisions that should be made consciously. Do you want to spend that freed-up technology budget on the more traditional, human-driven, creative aspect of marketing, or do you want to spend it on more high-end automation tools that can eke another few percentage points out of opportunities?

You could also take that 5 percent and invest it in your own technology team, building your own tools. As someone who runs a SaaS company in the PPC space—one that, rather than being an agency itself, provides services to agencies—I obviously love that model. Building your own technology can yield a much more defensible position in the industry. You can tell current and prospective clients you have your own, best-of-breed technology, which you yourself are able to maintain and keep developing. This is a very valuable thing to be able to say.

If, as is more probable, you buy existing technology rather than build your own, do thorough research. First, make sure you're not just buying something cookie-cutter off the shelf but instead get a tool that lets you automate your own agency's secret sauce, so you can scale your operations and manage more clients with your existing team. Then, do your best to use the full capabilities of the system you have put together.

Your agency's secret sauce will include how effectively you use such tools. This involves a unique value proposition that differentiates you from your competitors. Honestly, if everybody's buying Optmyzr software and running the accounts through that, and you're doing the same, then what are you selling as an agency? One thing you can sell is the fact that you're setting the tool up for optimum performance. In a tool like Optmyzr, there are so many custom settings that your secret sauce as an agency is going to be not that you use Optmyzr, but *how you use it to push your clients' accounts up to the next level.*

To take a simpler, more familiar example, with Excel you have to figure out what data to enter and how to process it. What is unique about your agency is not that you use Excel, but how you use it. The same holds true for technology vendors in the PPC space such as Optmyzr. Optmyzr will make recommendations about how to improve your accounts but also gives you greater control to tweak settings by asking different questions and taking different actions.

For example, if you wanted, you could have Optmyzr build an automation for bid management so you can hit return-on-ad-spend (ROAS) targets. That would be done by determining the average value of every click you get from the ad engine. Based on this historical data, rules could be written to set the correct bids for different segments, different devices, and so on.

However, it's far more interesting and valuable to push Optmyzr's capabilities to the next level by obtaining a client's data about margins and promotions, and feed that into the system as well. Now you could look not just at the value received from ad spends but the actual profitability generated by the products being sold through these ads. Most businesses would be very interested, because their goal is not making the most sales but the most profit. With whatever tool you buy off the shelf, the issue is really how you use it and how far you push it.

The power of customization lies in how you apply your unique business knowledge. You don't need to worry about the technology working. Concern yourself with asking the right questions, providing the right input, and knowing what kind of output to look for and when it's time to change tools. With PPC software, you can't just be a user. You have to become a power user. This is something both you and your clients should expect of your PPC agency.

WINNER TAKE ALL

One reason that the online advertising space is changing so rapidly—and your old value proposition is toast—is that it is now built on SaaS products that are very different from the software that, not so long ago, was sold as and installed from a CD. If you love the Office 2010 version of Excel, there's nothing to stop you from continuing to use it. You still have the disk it came on and you don't have to install any upgrades.

However, that kind of "the familiar ways are best" attitude is no longer possible with online marketing software of any kind. It's all done through the web and in the cloud. In the past year, Google Ads got rid of its old interface, making it no longer possible to use the old one. A number of features have changed dramatically in the new interface, which you have no choice but to use. In this increasingly familiar scenario, your old value proposition has to be toast, because you cannot continue to do the same thing that you were doing even a couple of years ago.

Because the technology is changing so rapidly and enabling entirely new approaches, it may be creating a winner-take-all market. Ten or fifteen years ago, you could be a successful PPC consultant if you had lots of local customers. This was meaningful, because you could meet your clients face-to-face to figure out their business needs and how to translate those insights into productive ads.

When I started at Google in 2002, video conferencing didn't really exist yet. Skype was around and worked off and on, but you certainly couldn't hook up multiple offices or do a very good screen share at the time.

Now, there are dozens of excellent, business-oriented video conferencing options. It no longer really matters where you are based. If you have an agency that has distinguished itself doing something in particular, people all across the globe will know and talk about it on social media. The winner now truly can take all.

A client may say, "I've heard of this guy, Kirk, who works out of Montana and is really good at shopping ads." There's nothing to stop your client from collaborating remotely with Kirk on a shopping campaign. This means there's nothing protecting you from long-distance competition anymore. A somewhat second-rate agency or consultancy might have been defensible in the past. The world has gotten so much smaller. You have to stay up with all the latest, because if you don't, somebody else will.

When doing PPC consulting, the job now to a large degree is to figure out how to be more successful than the hundreds of competitors who want to buy the same keywords. Old technology won't help because at least some of your competitors are going to have gone beyond that, using the latest and greatest. If they understand how to use the latest technology better than you can, you're at a competitive disadvantage.

Then word spreads on social media, and people know you're doing a no-better-than-average job, at least in part because you're not up on the latest technology. Both prospective and current clients may end up going with another agency or consultant, even one located in a different part of the world. This shift in how business is done is both relatively recent and enormous. It's critical to understand and face the issue of what you need to do to stay ahead of a game that has radically changed its rules. In this case, Google's recent announcements are correct: automation and machine learning are going to be critical to your business, and you need to build a strong message around them.

TO AUTOMATE OR NOT TO AUTOMATE

The question then becomes: what should and what shouldn't you automate? There's an easy way to think about this. If you can write something down for somebody else to do, then you can probably automate it. You can go to Upwork to outsource repetitive, tedious tasks of this kind. You simply communicate what step one, then step two, and then step three are. You can also communicate branching instructions: if in step two you find X, then do this; if you find Y, then do that.

What you're doing in a case like this is basically writing what programmers call pseudocode. Pseudocode uses a natural language—like English—to set down a series of instructions that a programmer can then turn into code. It could be thought of as a first draft of a computer program, the logic of which could be written by someone with no actual programming experience. The point is that you can automate many of your tasks and can actually take the first steps in doing so, even if you don't have a technology background.

The question then becomes: which tasks should you automate? The following graphic illustrates a way of looking at how automation can be prioritized.

WHAT SHOULD BE AUTOMATED

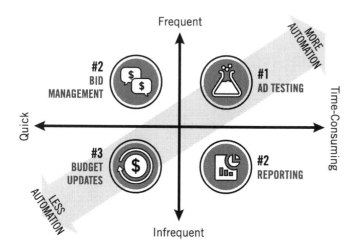

The vertical axis in this graph focuses on the frequency of the task. The horizontal axis focuses on how time-consuming the task is. Something that you do very frequently and is very time-consuming, like ad testing, should probably be automated first. Something that takes a lot of time but that you do less frequently, like reporting, should probably be automated next. Google Ads has already automated bid management, which is something done frequently and quickly. Things you don't do very often and that can be done quickly, like budget updates, are the last items you should consider automating. Automate them only if time and resources remain.

The creative aspects of PPC, such as writing ad text, which humans are better at than machines, shouldn't be automated. If you try to get machines to do creative, what they will come up with will be repetitive and undistinguished. Nevertheless, there's still a lot that goes into the creative side that can be automated if the overall task is broken down into its steps or components.

The first step in the process is getting the necessary data, and the second step is analyzing it: finding the winners and losers amongst previously tested ads, eliminating the losers, and using the winners as the basis for the creation of new ad texts. Now, many of these tasks could actually be automated. There's really only one task that can't be automated: taking what is proposed as the basis of a good, new variation and further crafting it. Even if a task can't be completely automated, there are still probably components of it that can, which will save you time to focus on the problems that you, as a PPC professional, do better than a machine.

AN INDISPENSABLE COMPLEMENT

Hal Varian, Google's chief economist, frequently gives the following advice to people starting their careers: "Seek to be an indispensable complement to something that's getting cheap and plentiful." This is also good advice for businesses. The question is: how is your agency going to complement the Smart systems that Google is making so cheap and abundant? Bid management has become commoditized and costs nothing with Google Ads's new technology. How do you make your agency complement Smart Bidding?

Again, look at what Google's already doing really well, and then help your clients figure out how to push it to the next level. The system is automated, but what is the machine looking at, and what may it be missing? How do you provide the missing data? What dials can you turn to make the system respond better to your client's on-the-ground business needs?

Another good example of an industry where this happened is analytics. As I've mentioned, I was a member of the Google team that acquired a small San Diego-based outfit called Urchin, which was then turned into Google Analytics. When the company made Google Analytics available for free, many people were afraid that this was going to kill the analytics industry. Chills went up the spines of all the vendors who were building analytics software and all the consultants and businesses helping others install analytics tracking systems.

What actually ended up happening is, because Google made analytics plentiful and cheap, all of a sudden everyone was paying attention to and able to afford analytics.

This turned out to be a huge boon for the analytics industry. Businesses that might not have been willing to invest in analytics software could now see how important it was and started to say, "This is something we should do more with. Maybe we need to hire someone with analytics expertise to help us."

It's the same with Google's Smart systems, including the most basic bid management. Google Smart Bidding has now automated the translation of target cost-per-acquisition (CPA) into maximum cost-per-click (CPC). However, that doesn't mean there's no work left to be done. The value you add is in determining how these automated systems can best be leveraged to achieve your clients' business goals.

TRADE-OFFS

If your agency wants to leverage rather than compete with AI, you also need to learn how to make sensible trade-offs. I've had several conversations with long-time Google product managers who say that many advertisers are bad at making these.

For instance, an advertiser might look at the search queries their ads are showing for and complain, "Google, you showed my ad for five searches that did not seem relevant to what we do." Advertisers then tend to have a knee-jerk reaction, changing their keyword type from broad match to exact match because they're disturbed Google showed their ad a handful of irrelevant times. However, if the advertiser is asked, "How many clicks did you get and how much money did you spend on these irrelevant impressions?" the response will often be, "Well, actually, zero."

The point is the advertiser didn't need to overreact to a few bad impressions. Google Smart Bidding will quickly pick up and learn, when using target CPA bidding, if some impressions are not driving the expected clicks or conversions. Adjustments will be made, and the number of bad impressions will go down. There may be a little bit of waste along the way, but advertisers and their agencies need to ask themselves if it is worth spending three hours manually pouring over all these query reports to find more negative keywords. Is the three hours of work you did worth more than the five dollars you might have saved?

The answer is quite obvious. A much better use of your time would be to set up an automated monitoring system to signal when performance dips below a certain level and, as a "pilot," to keep your eye on those higher-level signals and respond as necessary.

It's critical that an agency be able to explain the rationale for such trade-offs—that, for instance, it's unnecessarily costly and inefficient to try to suppress every single bad impression—to its clients. Yes, your clients may still have some strange or off-base sensitivities. Then, your job in your role as PPC "doctor" is to help the client understand what the cost/reward equation is. At that point, you've done your job well.

Your client may have hired your agency to manage their account for twenty hours a month for the next six months. Do they really want you to spend those twenty hours looking into what's going on with a hundred bad queries, or would they rather have you do something with more impact? Then you need to explain what the better use of your time and their money would be. That may well be *not* doing work that could be done as well or almost as well with machine learning, and instead doing work more associated with traditional marketing.

FUNDAMENTALS MATTER MORE THAN EVER

I've been a photographer since I was ten years old. I grew up at a time when we still used film. You would buy a roll with thirty-six exposures for seven bucks, which is considerably more in today's dollars. You shot that roll over a couple of days or weeks and then spent another twenty dollars to get the film developed before finally getting the prints back.

In those days, as far as I was concerned, there was no way I could permit myself to shoot bad photos. That was too expensive. I needed to frame and compose my shots using the "rule of thirds" and figure out how to get the lighting right. If things weren't just so, I'd never have another opportunity to take the exact same photo. I had to learn the fundamentals: the rules of composition and how to set the correct exposure.

At one point in my life, after the dot-com crash, I was a wedding and professional-event photographer. Digital cameras had just come out, so I bought an expensive digital camera and became the first and, for a short while, only digital wedding photographer in the Bay Area. I got jobs by telling prospective customers, "Listen, I've got this digital camera. I don't have to spend money on film, so I can shoot your whole wedding affordably and give you the digital 'negatives.' Then you can do what you want with them. I'll charge you much less than a typical wedding photographer would."

Today, most photographs are taken with cell phones. They take amazing photos, but at the same time, if the first shot isn't great, you can just take a hundred more. You keep going until you get the shot you want and then delete the other ninety-nine. There's really no extra cost to do that. Google's latest Pixel phone even takes hundreds of shots when you press the shutter and then uses AI to automatically recommend the best frame. The technology is now even doing the filtering for us!

For the most part, therefore, people don't need to know the fundamentals of photography anymore. They don't have to figure out how to do proper lighting or how depth of field can be used to create the blurry background effect that is so popular in a phone's portrait mode. Those features are built into their digital cell phone cameras.

However, that approach wouldn't have worked for me when I was a digital wedding photographer, and it still doesn't work in most professional contexts. Sure, I could have taken hundreds of pictures and erased 99 percent of them. But if I hadn't taken pictures of the bride and groom as rings were being exchanged, which were properly framed to show both the action and emotions critical to those exact moments, I would have failed. Random extensive coverage still can't account for what's most important.

PPC BASICS

The point is that the old-fashioned fundamentals remain important in most professional contexts in general, and in PPC advertising, in particular. Despite advances in digital automation, the experiment-and-see-what-sticks approach is a wasteful and bad way to do PPC. Experimenting with a PPC account remains an expensive proposition on which you are spending your clients' money. Unlike today's selfie photographers, you, as a PPC professional, have to know how to leverage modern tools to get the right results quickly, without doing a lot of throwaway work. Keep in mind, a truly great photographer will almost always take better photos than someone with an AI-infused Google camera. Mastery is still mastery.

One of the bid strategies offered by Google is target CPA. Say you have just hired a new account manager and tell them the client has a twenty-five-dollar cost-per-acquisition target. Do they actually know how the system processes the client's business goal to set the CPC bid that Google uses in its auctions? (It's expected conversion rate * target CPA, in case you were wondering.) If they don't know PPC fundamentals, they won't know that an expected change in conversion rate due to an upcoming sale is going to impact auctions during that time, and this may make your client vulnerable to competitors.

Even Google, despite all its announcements about turnkey machine learning systems, acknowledges how important basic knowledge still is, because they recommend adjusting CPA targets in anticipation of events like the one just described. The machine learning bidding system is trained on historical data and needs time to recognize when behaviors are shifting, a process that may take longer than the duration of the sale.

Say your e-commerce client is going to have the biggest sale of the year this coming weekend. Conversion rates are going to be much higher than normal during the sale.

However, as we've seen, Google machine learning might take three days to figure this out. By the time the system realizes that something has changed, it's too late; the sale is over.

If your agency has a strong process for ensuring every account manager is up-to-date on their PPC fundamentals, they'll know exactly what to do in this situation to make the client more successful. Machine and human can work together to produce the best results by translating this expected bump in conversion rates into a higher target CPA for the automated bidding system.

Yes, we are getting to a stage of increasing automation in which Google claims the "human factor" is becoming less critical—at least in certain respects. Yet this doesn't mean you no longer need to understand how the system works.

Thinking about the issue more broadly, you can ask yourself, "Why do we go to school to learn how to do basic addition? We all have calculators now." It's easy to ask your cell phone or say, "Alexa, what's five plus seven?" and get the right answer. You nevertheless still have to learn how to arrive at the answer on your own. If you're at the farmer's market and think the answer to the question is "fourteen," you'll easily overpay for the lettuce you're buying. There are many far more extreme situations where not being able to do basic addition unaided could lead to serious problems.

You have to know the fundamentals because, if you don't know how the pieces fit together and affect one another, your hands will be tied whenever you have to do something even a bit out of the ordinary. There are times when course corrections are needed, and at such times, it is dangerous to be on automatic pilot. You have to be a real pilot capable of taking over the controls.

GRANULAR TARGETING

With the increased importance of digital marketing, everything is becoming more quantified. This quantification also makes more granular targeting possible, and this brings with it a need for highly specific and creative messaging, something associated with the creative fundamentals of traditional marketing.

In earlier days, PPC did mass-marketing based on limited targeting capabilities, like the keywords a user searched on. Every decision had to be based on an average. There would be hundreds of thousands of searches on keywords like "buying flowers" every day. You basically ran one ad targeted to all those searches, because you didn't know anything more about the users who were making them. You also had one bid for all those searches, even though there are tremendous variations in how likely each click was to lead to a sale.

Now, if you've kept up with changes in Google Ads and understand the newest fundamentals like how audience targeting works in conjunction with keywords, you can do some things to set yourself apart. You know if these people have been to your website before. Are they existing customers? If so, are they high-value customers who buy from you frequently, or are they more Mother's Day-only flower purchasers? You know the user's demographics, such as gender, age, and household income. You also know what life stages or events might be coming up for the user. Perhaps she is about to get married, in which case your message should point out not only how beautiful but how economical your flowers are, since flowers for weddings are ridiculously expensive these days.

Knowing all this, you're no longer broadcasting a single message to everyone. If you produce a television commercial for national broadcast, both production and air-time costs are going to be high. You might spend a million dollars just producing the commercial. In such cases, you needed to send a message that will resonate with as many people as possible. That's not the case in PPC.

Even in its early days, online advertising permitted far more specificity: different ads for different keywords or locations. Now, we've arrived at the next level, and still more creativity is required in response. In the past, you were able to get by with just a handful of ads, but that's no longer true, given advances in targeting.

Optmyzr's auditing tool has a widget that will tell you how frequently you're repeating the same headline or call to action across all the ads in your account. It turns out that a large number of advertisers repeatedly use the exact same ad text components. In some cases, this may be a thoroughly tested, high-performing snippet of ad text. However, in many cases, the agency hasn't made the transition from one-ad-fits-all to writing text that more specifically targets and resonates with certain customer subsets. Being able to do this presents a great opportunity for today's advertisers.

An example of this is a locksmith advertising his services who wanted to find the highest-value customers. He figured that if someone is locked out of their car, they probably want to get back in pretty quickly. That's high value. The customer will be willing to pay more for the service. He then went further, targeting ads to people who searched on the keywords "get back into my locked car" on iPhones. People who buy iPhones typically have more disposable income. Finally, he decided to run those ads in response to searches made in sketchier neighborhoods where car jackings are more frequent. The locksmith was targeting people who were locked out of their cars in bad neighborhoods and had money to spend. He figured they would pay him a premium for his services, and he was right. While I'm not advocating doing what this advertiser did, since it is taking advantage of people in a tough situation, it does show an advertiser getting very creative in targeting a tightly defined microsegment.

Machine learning can now be deployed to find and categorize any number of microsegments, based either on criteria you supply or by recognizing patterns in data that you would have otherwise missed. You as an agency then need to make sure you've provided the system with enough ad-text variations to test which messages will resonate most with each of those segments.

Real-time analysis of and response to customer segments are the new reality. Think about users doing searches that indicate they intend to book a flight online. There are two or three different factors that might resonate. One user might be looking for the cheapest fare. Another user might be looking for the fastest flight: direct with no connections. A third user might be taking an international flight and looking for the greatest comfort, such as the nicest business class featuring private suites.

You've now arrived at three sensible, reasonably defined user segments and can write ads with value propositions that will resonate with each of them. However, you don't have to figure out which users making searches are in each of these segments. That's what the machine learning system will do. You just need to make sure you've given the system the content—text, graphics, videos—likely to connect with each user type.

THE SIXTH "P": PSYCHOLOGY

In June 2018, Google announced "Smart Shopping Campaigns." It is no longer necessary to build separate campaigns targeting search, display, and YouTube videos. You build a single campaign with various components, and the Smart Shopping system will figure out when and where to show the ads. As an example, the system will determine when an ad for your client's product should be placed next to a YouTube video that talks about a problem your product solves.

In other words, Google is handling "placement," one of traditional marketing's "five P's": product, price, placement, promotion, and people. That frees up your time to concentrate on other, equally important traditional marketing factors, such as product and pricing. Not having to worry about placement, you can spend more time doing, for example, in-depth competitive analysis that will ultimately give your client's product an edge over similar ones.

The creative aspect of advertising involves matching a product or service's value proposition with a call to action. The strong call to action closes the deal, but the deal won't even be considered unless you offer a value proposition that connects or resonates with users. People will only consider a call to action if the value proposition matches their values, desires, and needs. The value proposition needs to be relatable and believable.

What is "relatable" changes in different contexts, and there is a psychological aspect at play here. For instance, as previously mentioned, in a business setting, it's generally more appropriate to address "needs," and in a consumer setting to address "wants" or personal lifestyle decisions. Subtle word choices in your ad text will connect with different audience segments. Does the product or service meet a need the user literally can't live without or a desire for something that they're perhaps now able to afford for the first time?

You don't have to delve too deeply into user psychology, but the better you know your customer demographics and psychographics, the more interesting and appropriate your offerings can be. Companies used to just put their products out there in hopes they would connect with lots of consumers poised to buy. That's all changing, in good part because underlying business models and processes are also changing.

Optmyzr is a SaaS—software-as-a-service—business, and the trend throughout business today is to move to a subscription model. Several car manufacturers now offer automobile subscription services as well as leases. Perhaps Jenny likes to drive an SUV during the winter because she goes up into the mountains to ski. In April, when the snow has melted, she trades in her SUV for a sedan. In June, when the sun comes out, she trades that back in for a convertible.

Jimmy, on the other hand, is always looking for the most fuel-efficient vehicle, either because he's an environmentalist, wants to save money on fuel, or both. He will now be able to trade in his old vehicle whenever a more fuel-efficient model appears.

Understanding customer segments and patterns, companies can build products that better connect with consumers' needs. The better you understand the basic psychology behind what makes a consumer tick, the better you can target messaging. You can't quite get to the one-to-one level of communication yet, but, given micro-segmentation, you can get much closer to it than you could in the past.

Google Trends, which lets you see the prevalence of certain searches related to a certain vertical, provided a good example of this in a simple survey of the automotive vertical and the degrees to which people were searching for safety, fuel efficiency, and performance. When gas prices climbed, searches for fuel efficiency started to dominate. Most of the time, however, searches for safety dominated.

As a result, car manufacturers knew when their messaging should focus on their vehicles' fuel efficiency. However, even when gas prices are high, fuel efficiency doesn't matter most to everyone or even to most people. For certain customers, the importance of fuel efficiency might also be related to other factors, such as the automobile's pricing.

The point is, you can now start thinking more deeply about who you are trying to sell to. What message is going to connect with the psychology of a certain type of person? What used to be really difficult was figuring out which people fit into which segments, but machine learning is really good at matching the right message with the right user.

A classic example is Google's life-event targeting. You might think it would be easy to target people who are about to get married or just graduated from college. In fact, it's not all that difficult at a high level, because people who are about to get married are probably searching for "wedding cakes," "wedding florists," and the like. However, now that we are dealing with worldwide markets, there are cultural aspects to be considered that didn't come into the equation before. Wedding traditions in India are very different from those in the US. Even British weddings are different from American ones, and these differences are reflected in terminology, which impacts keywords and other search terms.

Machine learning is really good at finding patterns within large amounts of data. Who is searching for flowers, and are they about to get married or not? The machine learning system can identify these people and put them in different audiences. If your client is a florist, and the user who clicks on their ad is about to get married, the message should be: "We're able to do really big events with lots of flowers and bouquets." If the user isn't about to get married, the message would be more along the lines of how quickly a reasonably priced bouquet can be delivered.

PATTERN RECOGNITION

Of course, people are also able to find patterns, but to find them at anything like the granularity that a machine learning system can find them is either impossible or would take an inordinate amount of time. Your time is valuable, and it's probably cheaper and more effective for you to have a machine learning system deal with pattern-recognition and quantification problems.

However, what you as an agency need to understand is that all this quantification, pattern-recognition, and statistical analysis are a black box for most of your clients. Building a level of confidence is essential. The first time you as an agency utilize a machine learning system, you may be as much in the dark as your clients. By the second time you run it, you have the experience of having done it before.

Your job becomes taking on the doctor role and explaining to clients, "You may not understand how the computer does this segmenting, comes to these conclusions, and figures out the right bids. However, we've used this system and method for clients in just your situation, in the same vertical, with the same sort of problem, and here are the results that we saw. They were really good. That's why we're recommending that we go down this path." You're basically explaining what the machine learning system does at a high level, without needing to pinpoint exactly, on a technical level, what the system's algorithms do to produce one result rather than another.

Optmyzr uses machine learning in making geographic bid recommendations. However, if we run the same machine learning model twice in a row on the same dataset, we get slightly different results. They are not meaningfully different, but they are different, nevertheless. Clients sometimes pick up on this and ask, "Well, why is it that one time you tell me we should raise the bid by 7 percent and the next time, literally five seconds later, we should raise it by 8 percent?"

In machine learning, there is no strictly hard-coded path by which decisions are made. It's impossible, or at least very difficult, given the amount of analysis that would need to be done, to say why, at one point, the number 7.51 was arrived at and, at the next, the number 7.49. When that gets rounded, as it must because Google only accepts bid adjustments in increments of one, the first number shown to the user is eight, and the second number is seven. The point is that these answers are very close to one another, and this indicates how dependable the model is. If the system said 7 percent one moment and 15 percent the next, you would know you were working with a bad machine learning model.

This can be hard for people to understand. It also raises questions. "If you can't explain how the system came up with this answer, how do you know it's the right answer?" Looking at and finding patterns in huge amounts of data is something machine learning is able to do that is beyond our human capabilities. If your agency can at least explain what kind of machine learning model is being used and what factors it is looking at to make its inferences and predictions, you can put your client's mind at ease. If you've gone through the process for other clients with good results, you will be able to convince the current client to follow suit.

PROBLEM SOLVING

In getting back to fundamentals, always ask yourself what you're trying to achieve. Oftentimes, marketing is thought of as selling your product to someone, and that's fair enough. However, at AdWords, the goal was always more about solving a problem or filling a need someone has. Google Ads features very few of the lifestyle ads where you see happy people drinking beer to make you think, "Hey, I should get a beer, too." It's much more about: "We're about to have our third child and need a bigger, safer car." Of course, branding still comes into play—when you think safety, you tend to think Volvo—but you're basically filling a need.

PPC agencies sometimes get bogged down in the details: the spreadsheets, the math, and figuring things out. At the end of the day, it's important not to forget that you're basically trying to solve people's problems, and in doing so, creating happy customers and growing your clients' businesses. Happy customers are usually repeat customers.

If you are able to create repeat customers, you can now consider the customer's lifetime value, which means your client can afford to spend more money to acquire that customer in the first place. Being able to set higher bids will make you more competitive at auctions. Conversely, focusing on short-term sales ultimately makes your client less competitive as an advertiser.

The more finely tuned the system is, the better it is going to perform. Make sure you've set up all your tracking and other Google Analytics codes properly. Review them and decide when it is appropriate to take action and make a change.

The fundamentals are the foundation on which a PPC agency needs to be built. Now let's switch focus slightly, looking ahead to what it's going to take for your agency and its staff to endure, prosper, and grow in the machine learning era.

PREPARING YOUR WORKFORCE

Garry Kasparov, the first world chess champion to be defeated by a computer, IBM's Deep Blue, in 1997, offered some interesting insights into how humans and computers might work together most effectively, as Erik Brynjolfsson and Andrew McAfee relate in their book *The Second Machine Age*. He observed that a human player aided by a machine could beat a computer, and that when two human players were both aided by computers, a weaker human player with a better process could beat a stronger player with an inferior process.

Kasparov said, "The chess machine, Hydra, which is a chess-specific supercomputer like Deep Blue, was no match for a strong human player using a relatively weak laptop. Human strategic guidance combined with the tactical acuity of a computer was overwhelming." This has significant and very positive implications for your PPC agency or consultancy in the age of AI.

ROCK STARS AND OTHERS

Kasparov's quote echoes the theme that people and machine learning both have their own strengths—and weaknesses—and operate most effectively when working together. It also raises another point about team-building in a PPC agency or any other business. There is a lot of talk in the Silicon Valley tech world about "10X" performers: how a single great computer programmer, for instance, can do the work and have the impact of ten average programmers.

What Kasparov is implying in his statements about the importance of process is that, to succeed, you don't need a team entirely composed of Kasparov-type 10X "rock star" performers. This is a good thing, as it can be really hard to find only superstars to build your team.

Having a great process in place is oftentimes a bigger factor than who you hire. A good example is Starbucks, the biggest coffee chain in the world. Is Starbucks the biggest because they have the best baristas? They undoubtedly have some great baristas, but were they able to hire the

100,000 best baristas in the world? They couldn't possibly. What's made them so successful is their process.

An even more obvious example is the biggest fast-food chain in the world, McDonald's. Do they have the greatest cooks? Absolutely not, but they have an amazing process, and a great system and technology for cranking out burgers. Are these burgers the best in the world? Again, no, but the process the chain has put in place makes getting a tasty burger so quick and easy that people all over the world eat them at the rate, at last count, of 2.3 billion per year.

You can build a very successful agency by having amazing technology and other processes, and teaching your people how to use them to drive results. However, the converse—the need to hire people with specific skillsets—is also true.

In the past, you may have had to hire someone who could figure out what bids to set, someone good at math and spreadsheet work. But now Google does such a good job of setting bids, it's no longer necessary to hire someone with those skills. Instead, you want to hire someone with a strong process for figuring out what type of data needs to be input into the system for it to come up with the best possible bids. You also want to hire someone who has a strong grasp of different attribution models that weigh the relative importance of the various steps leading up to the final conversion or sale.

To differentiate itself, your agency needs to develop effective, efficient processes that enable you to deliver the best results as quickly as possible. A process is a related series of actions that are repeatable, scalable, and allow for quality assurance. You need employees who can follow processes, as well as continue to develop and improve upon them.

In the past, PPC agencies looked for scrappy self-starters who needed very little guidance after being told what the specific problem they needed to solve was. Today, however, the technology and tools are so good that it's critical to find people who have experience with those tools and know how to use them effectively.

ESSENTIAL SKILLSETS FOR TODAY AND TOMORROW

The skillsets you now need to hire for—and the skillsets you, your employees, and your prospective employees need to develop and continue developing—loosely equate to today's PPC tools. Your team should include people not only capable of working in Excel but also with analysis-oriented tools like R and Tableau, Google's BQML (Big Query Machine Learning), and third-party PPC automation tools like Optmyzr.

By the same token, the skillsets you will need to hire for tomorrow will equate to tomorrow's tools. To position yourself for the future, your employees will need to keep reskilling.

You also need people able to take a broader view. How does changing one part of a process change the process as a whole? What impact does a change to one system have on another system? How do all the components of a process stay coordinated and on track? Commercial pilots have a long process or checklist of things they need to go through before the plane takes off. The people you hire need attention to detail and the ability both to stay on track and put things in context.

In an age of constant change, it's vital to remain current. An Indonesian Lion Air passenger jet crashed into the Java Sea in October 2018, killing everyone aboard. The jet was the new model of the Boeing 737, the 737 Max. A manual pilot maneuver that would have worked to counter an erroneous sensor reading in the jet's previous models contributed to, rather than prevented, this tragedy when applied to the new model.

The upshot is that, as a "pilot," you need to keep your training up to date. Google systems change frequently, and when they change, significant, if rarely fatal, consequences can ensue, unless you've really kept up with how all the components of the system now interact with one another.

The doctor role also remains essential. Your agency needs employees with the Marcus Welby, MD bedside manner critical to dealing with clients. People in these roles need to have great social skills and be able to interact positively with clients, whether on the phone, in face-to-face meetings, or by email. Account managers also need to be able to think on their feet when a client throws them curveball questions.

The more specific skillsets you need to hire for, of course, depend on your value proposition and how you want to structure your agency. What are the human roles—doctor, pilot, teacher—that correlate to your specific offering? Having established your value proposition, the skills required to deliver on it should be fairly obvious.

Perhaps counter-intuitively, you should be careful about hiring someone who's been doing Google Ads for a long time. That is not necessarily a good quality, especially in people who haven't been consistently updating their skills. While lengthy Google Ads experience isn't necessarily a bad quality, quite a few people get very set in their ways. They have been trained in and love doing things manually, the way they used to be done in AdWords. They may not see the point of changing, because they feel that if it worked well enough in the past, it should work fine now.

In fact, things have changed dramatically, and this evolution is far from over. Your team has to be flexible and adaptable. They need to be ready for the game to change every two years, constantly learning, keeping up with what's new, and reskilling as needed. They must constantly question their own knowledge, because what worked two years ago is often no longer the best way to do it today.

In the past, moving around from job to job was seen as a negative. In today's environment, it could be a positive, because every time these people jumped around, they had to learn something new. Clearly, you don't want someone who has left a job because they couldn't gel with the others on their team. However, someone who is constantly looking for and adapting to change is a real positive in the PPC industry today.

HIRING AND TRAINING: BEST PRACTICES

To return to my own job history, I was trained as an electrical engineer and got a BS in the subject from Stanford. However, my first jobs at Google, which were basically to review ads and then do translation and handle Dutch customer support, had nothing to do with electrical engineering.

RESKILLING AGENCY PLAYERS FOR SUCCESS

What new skills do agency employees need? The usual answer is "programming," based on the logic that if machines are taking over jobs, people should learn how to create the machines. But that's wrong.

The proliferation of tool providers, in combination with how fast platforms are incorporating AI, means there's likely not a long-term need for an army of programmers at agencies. The new digital marketing job isn't a programmer, it's an "insight broker."

Insight brokers acutely understand what causes results and the right actions to take to produce different results. They're expert communicators who can sell ideas. They're world-class test designers. To fill these roles, people need to become experts in their clients' industries, root-cause analysis, marketing-mix modeling, testing methodology, and communication.

Does it make sense to hire these skills or reskill current employees? When hiring, you should assess candidates based on a mix of attitude and aptitude. Finding someone who scores high in both areas sounds great, but they are hard to find, expensive, and often in management positions. This means agencies need to choose people that are either higher aptitude or higher attitude.

High aptitude and low attitude people will have great performance, but they almost always become toxic. Your best bet is to hire people who are high attitude you can train. If you've done this, you have the right people on staff and thus, should focus on reskilling your team.

Reskilling employees requires a real investment of both time and money and should be a triangulation of self-teaching, conferences, and using case studies. Self-teaching means giving time to research topics by themselves or in small groups. Conferences allow people to learn entirely new and proven approaches, and case studies provide a hands-on way to learn, based on highly applicable situations.

Once your staff has acquired the knowledge, you need to transfer it to the team and new hires. Most agencies are bad at knowledge management, so this will require some work. Give employees the technical writing skills to capture knowledge, have a central location to store information, and a system for updating documentation.

JEFF ALLEN

PRESIDENT, HANAPIN MARKETING

Google's hiring premise was that it needed intelligent people who had proven by doing well in school that they could follow a process. Yes, it's true that people who didn't get great grades or even go to college at all can become extremely successful in all sorts of ventures. Many entrepreneurs fall into this category.

However, at Google, process was and is essential. Traditional schooling is basically a process, and people who know how to stick to that process get good grades. Standardized tests are another way to determine who can follow a process. These are all good, if not the only, ways to find people able to follow a company's process—whether Google's or your agency's.

Google knew that things were going to change quickly. If it was to accomplish its mission, it really had no clue what the people it was hiring at any given moment would be doing two years later. In the early days, the company certainly didn't know it was going to develop self-driving cars. Now they not only have a self-driving-car but a healthcare division. What they wanted was a workforce willing and able to adapt quickly, who find it fun and challenging to jump into new fields as required, while still being able to execute on current processes.

Your team must consist of people able to take a process and run with it, but here's where it gets a little tricky. You don't want those people to be just yes men and women blindly following a process that may be broken. You want them to speak up if something is not working. On the other hand, you don't want your team members to spend each and every day writing up notes on how your processes could be better. That's just as counterproductive.

Your team still has to go through the steps of the process and make sure things are getting done the way they should be done. Part of that can be automated, but you still need the pilot who sits in the plane for twelve hours, even if she is only flying it for eight minutes. During the other eleven hours and fifty-two minutes, the pilot still needs to pay attention to make sure everything is functioning properly. There's a specific personality type able to fulfill that particular role, providing yet another argument in the case against having a team entirely composed of rock star, top-gun fighter pilots.

In the early days of Google Ads, the team was actually not very big. The AdWords Editor was built by a core team of a product manager, three engineers, a user-experience designer, two representatives from the customer base, of which I was one, and a technical writer. This tool is used by virtually every large advertiser and manages ads worth billions of dollars a year. It was basically built by a tiny little team. Your agency doesn't necessarily need a huge staff, just the right people.

A successful PPC agency needs people who can take your baseline methodology and processes and get creative with them. Just remember that your old value proposition is toast. If you have great processes today, they're going to need to change, and your team needs to include people capable of both executing current processes and further developing your evolving value proposition.

CONCLUSION

My hope is this book has helped you better understand how machine learning, artificial intelligence, and automation are rapidly changing the world of PPC marketing. With this understanding, you can better formulate your own thinking on how you can position yourself to be able to stay and remain successful in the industry. Above all, I hope I've conveyed that our industry will continue to evolve at a rapid pace and that you will need to be ready to adapt to remain successful.

The skillsets where machine learning lags behind human ability—and may never surpass it in the future—include understanding your client's nuanced needs, creativity, and the ability to innovate. It's people, not machines, who come up with new ideas and experiments. By having a good sense of what has worked for similar campaigns in the past, PPC professionals can bypass the expensive experiments that a machine learning system would need to conduct to arrive at the same conclusion. If you're able to draw on your experience, you can save a lot of time and money.

The winners in the new world of PPC machine intelligence will be those who can take stock of advances in the technology and come to quick conclusions about their potential impact. Successful PPC professionals understand the businesses they're advertising for and the levers that impact those businesses. They now need to understand how digital marketing machine learning systems can integrate those unique levers to drive ever-better results.

What Google's Smart systems do is amazing and will be even more so in the future. Their optimizations, however impressive, are the "new ordinary." It is up to you to up the ante by bringing your own expertise and business data into the machine learning process.

Automated systems tend to look at averages in big datasets. Each of us is unique, however. Each account has its own tendencies and characteristics. It's well and good to look at averages and use them to help steer the ship. Ultimately, though, you also need to look as closely as you possibly can at what is unique to your situation and leverage that.

Sometimes there's not enough data to enable the machine learning system to function as intended. People can actually still make pretty good decisions even in the absence of "big data." We've been doing it for thousands and even millions of years. That's part of our human skillset.

So are empathy and the role of the "doctor." As a client service specialist who deeply understands your client's business and what might harm or benefit it, you can bring to bear an expert understanding of the range of solutions your clients need, as well as how to convey them.

As a "pilot," you will also play an oversight and monitoring role. As these new tools are put into play, you need to make sure they deliver on expectations. You have to set up the right alerts and a strong process to make sure campaigns stay on course. Also, because you should expect the unexpected, you'll have to make very quick decisions about what shifts in the competitive landscape mean and how they should be responded to. You will need to understand intuitively how to take evasive and perhaps even aggressive action.

If your skills lie somewhat more on the technical or quant side, there is a huge "teacher" role to be played in defining and developing the PPC machine learning systems of the future. These are not magical systems that just work by themselves, even though their ability to enable us to see things hard or impossible to see with the human eye alone may make them seem so. They had to be built by humans. These are still computer programs based on algorithms and statistical methods that people ultimately had to come up with.

Even if you aren't or don't want to be in the position of developing the newest machine learning systems, you need to understand the scope of the systems you work with. What kinds of data do they look at? What kinds of questions could they potentially answer? Then it's up to you to connect the dots by defining the important aspects of your clients' unique business data, so the system can do its magic in terms of managing bids, finding new customers to target, and doing a lot of other things it would be either impossible or too tedious to do manually. None of these things will happen if you don't play the role of "teacher" to the system in the first place.

Now go out and apply what you've learned to your Google Ads, Bing Ads, and other PPC accounts. Run experiments with different types of machine learning systems and begin to understand which ones perform better for certain scenarios and types of clients. At the same time, figure out how to rework your agency or consulting process to take account of this increasing automation, because you know that Moore's Law is bound to lead to an accelerating pace of improvement.

You almost certainly will need to rethink your whole process from start to finish. Something you used to do manually may no longer be necessary. It's up to you to experiment and determine which are the right tools for you and your clients. Try some systems you may have been either curious or skeptical about. Keep in mind, even if the tools are not as good as you would like them to be, the velocity of change and improvement is so high that you should be ready for a not-too-distant day in the future when the tool actually does what you need it to.

Then there is your agency's value proposition. A first step at revitalizing this is to understand which roles you and your team most enjoy playing and are especially good at. Figure out how you can best and most distinctively integrate PPC machine learning into your processes. Then set a strategy for selling your services: how to sign more clients and manage more accounts based on your new "people + machine" value proposition, the one advocated by Garry Kasparov.

As I've said many times, the landscape is evolving rapidly. I started thinking about writing this book in 2017. I feel the principles I've given you here will remain fundamentally true, but by the time you have read this, a few things may have shifted. If you'd like some help in keeping up with the latest trends, please take a look at my ongoing blog articles at Search Engine Land: https://

searchengineland.com/author/frederick-vallaeys. You can also follow my articles on the Optmyzr website blog: https://www.optmyzr.com/blog/.

Let go of your fear of future shock. Enjoy and benefit from the new age of machine learning in PPC marketing.

ACKNOWLEDGMENTS

First of all, I would like to acknowledge and thank my wife, Helen. By being so supportive of me and my entrepreneurial spirit, she made it possible for me to leave Google and start Optmyzr.

Of course, when I told her I wanted to start my own company, she said, "Great. Go do something else. But don't continue to do AdWords." I chose to ignore that advice and I think it was the right decision. There was still so much interesting work to be done with Google Ads, and I feel Optmyzr has been very useful for a lot of PPC professionals and agencies. But without Helen, there would be no Optmyzr.

Thanks to my kids, Ben, Zoe, and Elise, for allowing me to spend time on the road traveling the world to share my thoughts about PPC at conferences.

I'd also like to acknowledge my parents, Patrick and Marijke, for, among many other things, pushing me to get a tough electrical engineering degree from Stanford. This made me much better equipped to deal with all of today's technological changes, including marketing. And thanks to my sister, Charlotte. Having siblings fosters competitiveness, and that's helped me lead a better life.

Next, let me acknowledge my Optmyzr cofounders, Geetanjanli Tyagi and Manas Garg. After reading my Search Engine Land blogs, they got in touch with me, excited that I was doing something interesting, and proposed we start a company together. They are Optmyzr's lifeblood.

Thanks to the whole Optmyzr team for building useful tools and helping our clients improve their PPC optimizations: Shashank, Esperanza, Soumyajit, Dhiwakar, Akash, Haritha, Madhurima, Abhinesh, Julie, Juan, Dharan, Jeff, Aayushi, Raj, Matilde, Mirela, Minakshi, and Clara.

Of course, there are many people from Google and the early days of Google AdWords I am grateful to. They gave me my start in the PPC industry. It was fantastic to be able to have lunch with such smart people every day and discuss how we could make digital advertising better. Thank you to: Sheryl Sandberg, David Fischer, Emily White, Gap Kim, Bob Uttenreuther, Kirsten Nevill-Manning, Wesley Chan, Nick Fox, Jon Diorio, Richard Holden, Hannah

Mestel, John Maletis, Bryan Schreier, Griffin Golamco, Product Specialists, Ads Product Team, Ads Engineering, APE team, and parking-lot roller-hockey players. I know I can't list everyone here, but you know who you are, and you have my sincere gratitude.

Also, let me thank everyone at Search Engine Land, especially Danny Sullivan, Matt Van Wagner, Ginny Marvin, and Chris Sherman, for giving me a platform to share ideas about how we could all make the PPC industry better. One reason I like the PPC industry so much is that it's collaborative and there's so much opportunity. Even with supposed competitors, it doesn't really feel like you're competing. People are more than happy to share because everybody realizes that we're stronger together rather than trying to do everything ourselves. Great examples who should be followed of people always willing to share include: Larry Kim, Daniel Gilbert, Andy Taylor, Stasia Holdren, Mona Elesseily, Matt Umbro, Brad Geddes, Andrew Goodman, Eric Enge, Steve Hammer, and David Szetela. There are so many, and I know I'm forgetting people, but I'll acknowledge you in my next book!

I'd also like to acknowledge Joe Khoei, Emmanuel McCoy, and the team at SalesX. Joe acquired my consulting business and I remain on the SalesX board to this day. They keep me grounded and teach me what life is really like when you run a PPC agency.

Finally, I'd also like to acknowledge Tom Lane's editorial assistance and help in getting my thoughts out of my head and onto the page. I hope you have benefited from them.

Made in the USA
Columbia, SC
26 January 2020

87110873R00152